Mummy Cry-baby

Ellen McGovern

Typeset in Neuton

Design and publishing by Consilience Media

www.consil.co.uk

ISBN: 978-0-9573809-6-7

Acknowledgements

I would like to thank my family for their help, support and encouragement when I needed them most. And a special thanks to my brother Sean whom I do believe saved my life all those years ago. Also a huge thanks to my sister Margaret, for always being there with my best interests at heart, and also my sister Mary. And not forgetting my brother Chris and his late wife Hannah who were always there to keep an eye on me. Many thanks to you all.

Ellen

Chapter 1

On that cold March morning as I stood outside my home with my two small children and just one small case of clothes and some food for the babies, I had no idea what to do or where to go. The bailiffs had thrown us out onto the street and I had no idea where my husband was. Holding baby Steven in one arm and with Katie standing beside me, her arms wrapped around my legs and wanting to be picked up, I felt old and useless. My arms were aching, and the children were feeling cold and restless. Katie looked up at me and said, 'Mommy cry-baby.' That was something I would say when baby Steven cried. Now it was me doing the crying. How did I get to this point, I wondered?

I still think a lot about the past; I lie in bed and think how different things could have been, the happy family we could have been, and sometimes I feel I have lost part of my life that I can't ever get back. Now I can finally move on, though I do have many regrets, one of which is not having had more time to spend with my children when they were young.

I have read books and listened to songs about the young men who came to London to work, about how hard it was working long hours on motorways and building sites and so on; we all know the Irish were hard working men - though I have yet to hear anything about how hard the young women worked. Do they not deserve a little bit of recognition? They also had to work hard - sometimes rearing a family single handed, while their husband went straight to the pub to spend that hard earned money; so yes, if the men worked hard they also drank hard, and some of them forgot they had a wife and children at home to support. Those men were happy to let their wives do the providing, look after their children, have a meal ready for them when they decided to come home.

I am one of those women, so I know first-hand how hard it was, to earn enough money to pay the bills and feed the family, while being a mom as well. So yes, I do think those young women should be given a little bit of credit as well.

I was brought up on a farm a few miles from Dunmanway town, West Cork in Ireland. I have four brothers and three sisters. My grandfather's name was Danny Kelly; he was also a local farmer, and he had two children, John and Elizabeth. Elizabeth was always called Baby; John was my father. My Granddad was a lovely man. He was very kind to us as children. He was very much an outdoor person, and loved working on the land. He always cut the turf and saved it, making sure we had plenty for the winter. My dad never got on with his father; they argued a lot and I think that was because my dad was a bit lazy when it came to farming – he had no interest in the land. His great passion was horses: he always kept two or sometimes three; if the work on the farm involved horses, he would gladly spend his time working, ploughing, harrowing and so on.

Granddad sold his farm in the late 1940s. He was paid £500 for it. Both he and my grandmother came to live in our house. Gran was also a lovely person; she was a big woman and had problems with her walking. Mom often told us what a great help she was when we were young. Nana's maiden name was Margaret McCarthy and she came from a place called Grawn, about ten miles from where we lived.

She was one of eleven children. We never had much contact with her family, as they all moved to different parts of the county; we knew of them but never got to know them. My Gran died on 28 November 1956. And granddad passed away four years later; they were both eighty-four when they died. My mother's maiden name was Mary Buckley. She came from a place near Johnstown – I suppose you could call it a village: it had two shops, a pub and a post-office. My Grandmother's maiden name was Ellen Healy. I never knew her as she had died before my mom got married; she suffered from Arthritis for many years and died in her early sixties. She had one brother called John. Granddad on my mother's side was Johnny Buckley. He had spent many years in America, and I don't know anything about his background – I wish I had asked my mom more questions about her parents, when she was alive.

I know he bought our farm when he returned from America and had a new house built on the land. He married my Nan Ellen Healy in 1912. My mother was born two years later in 1914. She was an only child and was christened Mary Ellen Buckley. Mom and Dad married in the Catholic Church in Johnstown in the Parish of Kilmichael in 1940. I'm not sure how they met, but Dad often told us that Mom only married him after she'd seen him swimming. Mom would smile and say hush John, don't be telling stories like that to the children. We all knew it was one of his stories, because Dad could not swim. Dad and Mom had a great relationship: she adored him and he her; there were never any major arguments that I can remember. Mom was a very kind and gentle person – she wouldn't say boo to anyone, she hated to see anyone upset, and would wait on my dad hand and foot.

Their first son was born in 1943, and was named Daniel Christopher, but he was always called Chris. Irish people swap and change names, and are rarely called what is on their birth certificate. My sister Margaret Mary was next in arriving. I was born on 12 September 1946 and was christened Ellen Philomena. I did not know until I got married that this was my real name, as I was always called Eileen. My brother Sean was born on 7 April 1948. Sean and I were always very close and we looked very much alike - neither of us was blessed with good looks. Mary Gerard was born on 28 August 1953. She was always called Mary going to school. When she came to London, she changed her name completely and is now called Geraldine. See what I mean about the Irish and their names? The first five of us were called after our parents and grand-parents. By the time my younger brother was born on 30 March 1956 I think my mother was running out of names, so he was called Francis Joseph. I was ten years old and I remember Mom and Dad bringing him home from hospital. He was so small and cute we were all delighted with him. He suffered with convulsions as a baby but grew out of them when he was about four. We all had to be very careful with him. Florence Anthony was the baby of the family. He was born on 12 March 1957. We have always called him Flur, so the names are still changing.

My Mom, Dad, grandparents and seven of us all crammed into our three bedroom house; there were two double beds in two of the rooms, and one bed in the other room. That was my grandparents' room. There were two rooms downstairs: one was the parlour which never got used, and the other was a large kitchen where everything went on - cooking, eating, sitting, playing. I even remember Dad bringing a horse in there to shoe, when it was raining outside, though we did have a stable. Dad was a happy-go-lucky sort of person; he would sing 'Red is the Rose', 'Skibbareen' and on occasions 'The Boys of Kilmichael', which of course was a rebel song. He could sing many songs but never knew all the words, so all we got was a verse of each one. One of his favourites was 'Come and sit by my side if you love me'. He would invite Mom to sit on his knee; she usually did so with a big grin on her face.

My mother was a very loving, caring person; anything she did for us or Dad was never too much trouble. It must have been hard work keeping seven of us under control, washing, cooking and all the other chores that had to be done daily. When we were young children all the cooking was done on an open fire. I remember one time when Mom was in hospital, Dad was doing the cooking. He made bread and put it in the bastible over the fire with coals on top of the lid. After about a half-hour the lid started lifting and he soon realised he had put too much dough in the pot. We thought it was very funny. Soon after we got an electric cooker.

Dad and Mom were a very close, united couple; I never heard them say anything bad about each other. Years later when I got married, I often thought of them, when I was being sexually and mentally abused by my husband, the man that was supposed to love me.

One of my first memories as a child was when I started school. The school was about two miles away, and the only way to get there was to walk with my older brother and sister, Chris and Margaret. Sometimes we would take a short cut across the fields. On one occasion there was corn growing in the field near the house and we made a path through the middle; we sat down for a while and I fell asleep. Chris and Margaret ran off home and forgot about me. When Dad noticed I was missing he asked them where Ellen was. They were reluctant to say because they would get told off for going through the corn field.

When I was three years old I fell into the open fire, and was badly burned - my right hand, it was burned up to my elbow. Mom told me years later, that she had been out milking when she heard my Nan screaming for help; when my mom got to the house she found Nan outside holding me with my hand in a barrel of water. Mom went on horseback to the Post Office to phone for a doctor; when he arrived he cut the blisters and bandaged my hand and arm. Mom told me my arm was in a sling for many weeks. My arm is still badly scarred, but it has never bothered me. Dad would say, with a mark like that Ellen, you will never get lost.

As young children, growing up on a farm was fun: we would play out in the fields; go fishing with jam jars in the nearby river; we would kick football and play shops. There were plenty of things around the house, farmyard, and fields to keep us occupied. Mom would be out calling us to come indoors when it started to get dark. We would have our supper, say the rosary and it was time for bed. Even saying the rosary was fun - one of us would always find something to giggle about, and the rest of us would follow. Mom was a very religious person and would not approve of such behaviour; she would tell us off and say God is watching, and he won't forgive you, but that truth did not stop us messing around during the rosary.

As children we were a happy bunch but we all had our jobs to do after school, anything from milking the cows, to getting buckets of water from the spring well down the lane, and feeding the chickens, hens, turkeys and horses. Dad would cut and bring home the firs; we would put it through the crusher and put it in the stable for the horses. There were always disputes about who was to do what job; we all had our likes and dislikes.

Saturday was a busy day in our house. The stairs would be

scrubbed and the kitchen cleaned. In the evening the shoes would be polished - that was a job none of us liked. Mom would have all our best clothes ready for us to wear on Sunday morning for Mass. Dad would tackle the horse and cart; he and Mom would sit in the front, and all of us would climb into the back. There were very few motorists at that time; anyone who had a car, we thought they were very rich, which we were not - Dad and Mom didn't have much money, but we were all well fed and smartly dressed. Mom was very good at sewing, knitting and darning Dad's socks. We wore a school uniform and that helped save our other clothes.

Saturday night was bath night for us children. Dad would have two kettles of water boiling by the fire, and Mom would get the big iron bath, fill it and in we would go, one by one, the girls first then the boys. Dad always dried our hair; he would put us lying across his lap in front of the fire.

I have so many fond memories of that little spot in the South of Ireland, the fun we had when the hay and corn were being cut and saved, chasing each other around the stacks, jumping over them, knocking them down, Dad shouting at us. He would say if you can't help, go indoors and help your mother. The day of the trashing was a real special time; we would be allowed to stay off school, and it was wonderful watching the trashing machine working. My older brother Chris was allowed to help and the rest of us would help Mom in the kitchen, to prepare food for all the men. The neighbours all helped each other during the trashing season.

As we got older we were allowed to ride the horses (the quiet ones); being on horseback was nothing new to us: Dad would put us on as soon as we could sit up and hold on. I especially loved the horses. To begin with Dad would catch the horse and help us on.

Dad never used a saddle - I don't even remember if we had one. I had many falls when out riding; I loved galloping, and could not resist the odd jump, so I often ended up on the ground.

Ballabuigh Races and Horse Fair was a very special time for all the family; it was held on August Bank Holiday in Dunmanway, and we were allowed to go. It was a special time for dad too; he would often be selling or buying a horse. He would always end up drunk. Mom did not like the horse fair; she would worry about Dad getting drunk, getting involved in fights or wasting his money on another horse, that we did not need. In fact Ballabuigh was Mom's worst nightmare. Dad didn't usually drink very much - sometimes he would go for one pint after Mass on Sunday, but the horse fair was different and he would always get drunk.

Chapter 2

Years later when I lived in London, I would always
to Dunmanway for Ballybuigh; it had always been   .. place
for me.

My brother Chris was the first one of the family to go to
London in 1959. He was 17 years old; he lived with John and Aggie
Coughlan at 21 St Cuthbert's Road, Cricklewood. They were
relatives of our family. He was happy living there, and soon found
a job in a timber yard, where he learned to be a carpenter. He sent
money home every week, until he got married in 1966. After his
first year in London he came home for a holiday, and asked me
to go back with him. Mom and Dad raised no objections, as I had
already been working and living in the Convent in Dunmanway,
coming home at weekends - so the idea of going to London with
Chris was great.

My auntie 'baby' as she was called, had a son living at 159
Falloden Way, Finchley. It was arranged for me to live there. In
August 1960 I left home with my brother Chris; I was very sad
leaving my younger siblings and Mom and Dad. We got the bus
from Dunmanway town to take us to Cork City bus station; from
there to the ship, the 'Innisfallen', was walking distance.

I had had a terrible fear of water ever since I had jumped into
a flooded river, years earlier on my way home from school. It was
one of our shortcuts; instead of walking further along the road
to the bridge, we would jump across the river and walk through
the fields. On this occasion Chris and Margaret had got across. I
threw my coat to them but they didn't catch it, and it ended up in
the river, which is why I went in to get it, and was washed down

river by the floods. A branch of a tree stopped me and I was able to scramble out - ever since then I have had a great fear of water; the iron bath in front of the fire was enough water for me.

So seeing that ship and all the water scared me, and I cried all the way to Fishguard, pleading with Chris to take me back home. He said if you shut up, Ellen, I will take you home at Christmas. The boat was very rough and most of the people were sea sick, including me. The toilets were covered in vomit and everywhere we walked was the same. There were few seats, so we were unlucky and had to sit on the floor. Arriving in Fishguard nine hours later, I was oh so pleased to get off that ship, as Chris and I got to the railway station in Fishguard to catch a train to London. I asked, "When you take me home at Christmas can we go by plane?" He smiled and said you have to earn lots of money to go on the plane, and he was right, so on my next visit to Cork, it was back on the Innisfallen again. I never liked it and was always seasick. But I was going home and that made it bearable.

My first night in London was spent at 21 St Cuthbert's Road with John and Aggie Coughlan who owned the big four storey property. They kept lodgers in the top two floors; Chris and John's brother shared a room in the basement. John and Agnes had no children so Chris was their blue-eyed boy. He was like a son to them. The next day my Cousin Rickie arrived to take me to his home in Finchley. I did not know him very well, and had never met his wife Joyce. Ricky was already in London when we were growing up, and Joyce was English-born. Those people were strangers to me, and I knew Chris wouldn't be with me. Ricky and Joyce treated me well. They lived in a two bedroom house with the sitting room upstairs, and a dining room and kitchen on the ground floor; the bath was in the kitchen, covered over with a work top; the toilet was outside the back door.

The day after I arrived, Joyce took me to a small shopping place near where they lived; it was called the Market Place. Joyce said I needed to get a job. There was a big Woolworths in the market place; we went in and Joyce asked if they had any vacancies. After a short interview I got the job on the biscuit and sweet counter, which sounded great, but because I was only fifteen, the wage was only six pounds a week. I paid Ricky £2 a week for my keep and £2 was sent home to Mom. After working there for a few months, the manager offered me a job in the office, which I accepted. The wages were much better, but I soon realised that being closed in an office all day was not for me, so I left the job. I found my way back to Cricklewood and St Cuthbert's Road. Aggie invited me to stay for the weekend, so I could go to the Galtymore with Chris; she had made up a bed for me in the sitting room.

The Galtymore was the biggest and best Irish Club in London. It was a meeting place for the Irish and I loved going there on weekends. I got to know other girls staying at no 21 and I started going out with them. I think Chris was pleased about that, as I had been like his shadow since arriving in London.

Finding a new job was easy at that time: you could change your job every day if you wished. My next job was in Heinz Food Factory in Park Royal; the work was easy, packing tins of all kinds of food, off a conveyer belt into boxes. I made new friends and was happy; though I missed my home I wasn't so homesick any more.

My sister Margaret came to London in 1962. A double room had become available in 21 St Cuthbert's Road, and as I was spending every weekend there, Agnes said Margaret and I could have the room for £4 a week. I was really happy to have Margaret with me and for the first year we went everywhere together. Margaret got a job in Smiths Industries in Cricklewood. They assembled clocks. It was a huge factory which employed thousands of men and women. I later left Heinz and went to work for the same company.

Our social life was really good back then; we would go out Friday, Saturday and Sunday nights, mainly to the Galtymore which had two dance halls. Kilburn also had two Irish Clubs, The Bemba and the National, where we would sometimes go. We would always go back to Cork once or twice a year. Mom, Dad and our younger brothers and sisters would be delighted to see us, and be eager to see what presents we had brought for them.

Chapter 3

It was in the summer of 1963 that I met Harry, the man who was later to become my husband and tormenter. I first met him in Woolworths in Cricklewood Broadway. I would often have my lunch in the store - it had a tea and sandwich bar. He was also having lunch and started chatting to me. He seemed to be a nice person and I would often see him there in the weeks that followed. Then one night I met him in a dance hall and we had a few dances. He had asked me out on a date before this meeting and I had said no, but when he offered me a lift home in his car I accepted, and on the way home he asked if I would go out the next weekend with him - and that is where the relationship started. I enjoyed his company and he was kind to me; he would take me to the pubs and to different venues around London.

He came from Co Roscommon, and had been living in London for seven years. He never spoke much about his family in Ireland, only that he had two sisters who lived in Wembley. He also told me that he had been engaged to a girl from Co Mayo and they had a baby son, and that she had left him for another man. He did not have contact with her or his son any more. I was surprised to know this girl had a baby before she got married and shocked that she then left the baby's father for another man. This did not make sense to me, and I was not sure if I should believe Harry's story or not. At seventeen I did not have any experience of boyfriends; there was no sex education in school and it was a taboo subject in our house. I remember once when we were all at home, Chris, Margaret and I were standing at the bottom of the stairs in the hallway. Chris said he had a secret to tell us; we were about eleven,

nine and eight. He said Mrs Carroll was in calf because she had a
big belly; she was a neighbour. Mom was listening upstairs; she
came down and hit Chris a smack around the side of the head. She
was really cross with him saying how sinful it was to talk about
such things. So when I came to London I was totally naive about
the facts of life and what went on in the real world.

The catholic religion played a big part in my life as I was
growing up. My mother was a very religious person. She would
pray to all the saints for different reasons; it would be St Antony
if she lost something – and she often did, so St Antony was always
on call at our house. Mother would recite the 10 commandments,
the seven deadly sins; we would also be reminded that there was
Hell and Heaven – if we were good and did not commit any of the
deadly sins, we would go to Heaven. I could never be as holy as my
Mom, but I did go to church every Sunday in Kilburn. Although
I did not say the rosary in the evenings, I always tried to say a few
prayers. Years later when I was in trouble and I really needed God's
help, he wasn't there for me. My friend Rita, a girl I used to work
with, would say to me, 'Ellen, there are people a lot worse off than
you in the world and there is only one God, so you have to wait
your turn.' As the weeks turned into months and months turned
into years nothing much changed; I was still very unhappy.
My life was nothing like I had hoped it would be. With a strict
Catholic upbringing and a Mom and a Dad whom I didn't want to
upset or disappoint I carried on in the hope that one day things
would change.

As I continued to date Harry, he would pick me up at weekends
and take me to different places around London. He liked to
have a drink and would encourage me to have a drink also; he
would buy Babysham, gin and other drinks to see if I liked any

of them. I would say stop wasting your money and get me coke or lemonade. His friend Mick Glen would often be with us. I did not like him much; I found him very abusive and rude to people. They would often go to a cafe after a night out. Sometimes I would ask Harry to drop me home first and he was usually agreeable. As the months went by Harry and I spent more time together. He would call for me on Saturday when I was not working and take me out in the lorry. I loved being in the lorry; I felt on top of the world, looking down on everyone.

We would often meet up with my brother Chris and my sister Margaret in the Galtymore. They seemed to like Harry as I did. He would talk about the future saying, 'Ellen, when you are a bit older we'll get married.' At that stage of our relationship I had no interest in getting married; I was not even eighteen yet and he was twenty four. I thought it was a bit odd that he made such a statement; after all I had only been going out with him for a short time.

One night after we had been to the dance with his friend, Mick suggested we should go to the café at the bus station for something to eat. Harry said I should go along with them as this place was in Cricklewood and still near home. As we got there the cafe was closing; the person in charge said, 'Sorry we can't serve you now.' After trying a little polite persuasion and getting nowhere, they changed their tactic; they started shouting and swearing at the manager, telling him where he could put his food. I was shocked at the way they were behaving; I could not see any sense in their attitude as the place was closing. The manager said he would call the police; they left with me in tow.

We got back in the car and Mick said we would go to the Ace cafe. Harry agreed and said, 'Ellen, you will like it there, that's where all the Bikers go. The place is open all night and it's not far from here.' As we arrived I could see all the motorbikes and these people were all wearing leathers with Hells Angels written on their jackets. They were everywhere and I felt very insecure. As we queued at the counter the police arrived and arrested Harry and Mick for their abusive language and threatening behaviour at the bus station café. I was upset and frightened, not knowing how to get home, and being left on my own with all those bikers. Harry asked one of the police officers if he could ring someone to pick me up; looking at me the officer could see how scared I was, so he agreed. Harry rang somebody and said to me, 'Don't be scared, someone is going to pick you up – his name is Joe Flynn. Stay inside the door until he comes.' Then the police took them both away.

I stood there scared of the bikers and also worried about this man that was coming to take me home. I had never heard Harry talk about this person. I wondered for how long he knew him, and how he would recognise me, and what if he did not turn up? I stood there for what seemed like ages, then a man came towards me and said, 'Hello, are you waiting for a lift home?' Before I could say anything he asked, 'Are you ok? I am Joe Flynn – Harry rang me.' On the way back to Cricklewood, Joe asked me what had happened, and I told him. He asked me how old I was. I said, 'Seventeen.' Shaking his head he said, 'Take my advice and stop hanging around with them two Assholes, I know them well.' As I got out of his car at no 21 saying 'thank you for bringing me home', he said, 'Remember what I told you.'

I avoided Harry for the next couple of weeks. I knew he was out of order for behaving the way he did, and as the weeks passed I did not think much about Harry, though I did wonder how they got on with the police that night. The next time I met him was in the Galtymore club. Big Tom and his band were playing there. My brother Chris and my sister Margaret were also there. There was always a big crowd in the Galty when Big Tom was playing; it was easy to get lost on such nights. So, when I saw Harry in the Celia Hall I went into the other Hall where Big Tom was playing.

We had a great night, but as we queued to get our coats and leave, Harry was standing inside the door as I walked past. He joined me and said, 'Are you trying to avoid me?' As we walked he said, 'I want to talk to you, I will drop you home and we can talk.' I said, 'As you did the last time.' He said, 'You got home safe, didn't you?' He apologised for what had happened and said, 'Nothing like that will ever occur again. Please come out with me next weekend – I will take you somewhere nice, and we will go and visit my sister.'

Harry never spoke about his family, though he had told me he had two sisters, so I accepted his apology and said I would see him next weekend. Harry had never said much about his parents or where he came from in Roscommon; though I would often ask him, he was never forthcoming with information about his home. I thought that was very odd as I talked non-stop about my family; he knew everything about me and where I came from, even the number of animals we had on the farm. He would want to know everything but gave little or no information about himself, as I was to discover years later, when our son and his wife went to Ireland touring, and the address Harry had given us was incorrect. They spoke to many people in the neighbourhood, but could find no evidence of a McGovern family ever living there.

As I continued to date Harry I found him very possessive of me. He would want to know everything about my work, who I worked with, what we talked about, when we were out together if a man spoke to me that he did not know, he would want to know who he was, where I'd met him, had I ever been out with him. As I was to learn you get those warning signs, but don't heed them, because you want to think the best of the person you love.

Harry had been putting pressure on me to have sex with him. I was not ready for the intimate side of the relationship at that time, and I would say to him sex is for married couples, and it is a sin to have sex before marriage, and I really believed that. He had different ideas, and said that was rubbish, and if I loved him and he loved me it wasn't a sin. I still said no and told him that if that was all he wanted me for he could go, and I did not want to go out with him again. He then said, 'I love you, so I'm happy to wait - but Ellen, don't let your religion come between us.'

One weekend, a short time after that conversation, Harry raped me. It was one night after we had been out for a drink. I was so upset and all he could say after was 'you're mine now and don't be mad at me'. But I was mad at him - he had no right to do such a thing to me. I was crying and swearing at him, so he said, 'Sorry, I had better take you home.' The next couple of weeks I was very stressed, worried in case I could be pregnant. I loved Harry but did not want to commit to him in this way, and if this was the way he was going to behave I would not want to be with him anyway - but he had taken away any chance I had of meeting someone else. Back in the sixties I believed a woman only had sex with one man and that would be her husband. I felt trapped and used, and for some reason I blamed myself for being so trusting and naive.

Chapter 4

My sister Margaret and I went to Cork that summer for our usual two week holiday. Mom had not been well, so Dad asked one of us to stay and help out until Mom was feeling better. It was decided that I should stay; I was pleased about that. I had not told Margaret or Chris what Harry had done to me. I thought they wouldn't understand, maybe they would think it was my fault, and what if they told Mom or Dad? So I felt I had to keep quiet and tell no one.

I loved being home with my younger brothers and sisters, doing the housework, and other jobs around the farm yard. My brother Sean was still at home. He was one year younger than me. We would go out together at the weekends, we would visit a neighbour's house where we would play cards, or sometimes we would go dancing to the local Platform. It was nice there in the summer, being an outdoor event.

Money was scarce and sometimes we wouldn't have enough to get us into the Dance Hall in town. Mom would give us what she could afford, but it would not be very much. Sean and I came up with a plan of how to earn extra money. We had lots of hens at the time, and when we collected the eggs from the nests around the farm yard, we would hide some each day. When the weekend came, we would have two dozen to sell at one of our local shops. That was Sean's job, so our plan was working well and we always had money for the weekend. Mom was getting concerned about the lack of eggs, and would say, 'I think them hens must have found a new nest, or they're not laying as many eggs as they used to', so Sean and I decided we could manage with a lesser income –

but it was good while it lasted.

Sean's friend Danny would often give us a lift home from the dances; his family lived local, and I remembered him from school days though I never remember him going to school. He was 10 years older than me; we would walk past his house and he would often stop whatever he was doing to talk to us. He was still the same friendly person that I remember from back then; he would often dance with me, and he would want to know things about London, about my job, my social life and whether or not I would go back there. Then he asked me out on a date and I said yes. I told Danny about the boyfriend I was going out with in London - not everything: I couldn't tell him my dark secret, thinking if I did maybe he would not want to go out with me. Danny and I spent a lot of time together over the next few months. I really liked him; he was always good to me, and always the perfect gentleman.

As the months went by, and Mom was back on her feet, I knew I would have to get work in Ireland or go back to London. Danny wanted me to stay and said I should apply for jobs in Cork City; he had family living there, and said I could stay with them. My dad found out I was dating Danny, and he went mad, and said, 'While you are living under my roof you will do as I tell you, you will not go out with this man again.' I tried to tell Dad how much I liked him, and how good he was to me, but he wouldn't listen, so when I didn't turn up to meet Danny that weekend, he came up to the house to pick me up. Dad went outside to talk to him; he said, 'My daughter won't be seeing you again, so you keep away from her.' I was upset and very angry with Dad - after all I had been living in London for the past two years, and now he thinks he can forbid me to go out.

Dad was a great man to hold a grudge. He had fallen out with Danny's father some years ago; I did not know what that was about, but I knew Dad had a temper and sometimes would fall out with people for no good reason, and if he didn't like one member of a family, he then wouldn't have anything to do with any of them. My brother Sean came up with a plan: as I wasn't allowed to go out, we would wait until everyone had gone to bed and when we heard Dad snoring, we would go out the back window at the top of the stairs, Sean first and he would lift me down, but then it wasn't as easy to climb back in, so we got our younger sister Mary to go downstairs, and unlock the front door, so we could get back in. If anyone heard her, she would say she needed a drink of water.

I continued to see Danny, and made plans to get a job in the City, which was 35 miles away. Dad would never know if I was still seeing him or not. Mom had no concerns about me going out with Danny. She would have been happy to see me settled down in Ireland; she did not want me to go back to London. I was quite happy to stay in Ireland, but I knew sooner or later I would have to tell Danny what Harry had done to me in London. I wanted to tell him, but I worried about what he might think - would he still feel the same, or maybe he wouldn't want to have any more to do with me. Thinking I would be best to wait until I got a job and moved to the City, I would tell him then and that was something I wasn't looking forward to.

Dad found out what Sean and I got up to, and he was livid, telling me, 'You're going back to London next week, you are better off over there with Chris and Margaret. Now I don't want another word from you. I will arrange for someone to take you to town and put you on the bus to the City on Monday.' I was shocked and upset and thought, how could my dad do this to me?

I asked Sean to go and see Danny and tell him what was happening, and that I would write to him from London. Mom was very upset; she was crying. I hate to see my mom cry. Dad had not changed his mind, and when Monday came I set off. Sean went to town with me to catch our bus. He could see I didn't want to go and said, 'Don't worry Ellen, you will be home again this evening.' I said, 'What do you mean?' and he said, 'You will see'. We got into town and there, parked behind the bus, was Danny. I was delighted to see him. He said, 'You are not getting on that bus; I am driving you to Cork City.' So that's what Sean meant. We talked a lot about the situation, on our way to Cork. I asked Danny to come with me, but he said his dad was getting on in years and he wasn't very well, so he couldn't leave and go to London at that time. Then he said, 'You are not going away; we will spend the day around the City, and do some visiting, and I will take you back home this evening. You can say you missed the boat. Your dad might have calmed down by then.' However, Dad had not changed his mind. He was surprised to see me back, and after spending the next 10 minutes lying to him, he said, 'You will have to leave earlier on Wednesday and make sure you don't miss that boat.' So I left and did not contact Danny again. I don't know if we would ever have made it up the aisle. If Dad hadn't been so small minded, and if I were a bit older, if I was more determined, so many ifs...

Chapter 5

Back in London everything was the same as when I left. It was good to see Chris and Margaret again. I got my old job back, and soon accepted that I would have to get on with my life in London. Chris had met a nice girl; she came from Kilogarn in Co Kerry. Her name was Hannah Murphy and she would become his wife two years later. We all liked Hannah; she was every helpful and straight talking – if she did not agree with something, she wasn't shy with letting you know.

I had met up with my old flame Harry within a few weeks of returning from Ireland. He was pleased to see me, saying we were meant to be together, and how much he loved me and missed me. Harry was a real ladies' man, back then a real charmer, so we were back together and a few months later he asked me to marry him, and I said yes. He bought me a ring in H Samuel's jewellers in Kilburn, so we were engaged. I did love him and felt sure he loved me. I still believed I was damaged goods, and maybe no one else would have me, which of course wasn't true. I was very naïve back then and believed sex before marriage was a great sin, and girls were virgins when they got married – which I later learned was a myth.

Harry would often say to me, if I can't marry you, then I won't marry anyone, which I found quite sweet, until he would go on to remind me that I was his. 'You know what I mean,' he would say, and I did. I would remember the 10 commandments, that Mom would have drilled into us, and though it wasn't my fault I had committed a huge sin. How silly I was.

My brother Chris and his girlfriend Hannah had also got

engaged, and were planning their wedding, which was to be held in the Sacred Heart Church, Quex Road, Kilburn, on 12 March 1966. As our family would be coming from Ireland for his wedding, Harry and I thought it would be nice if we could arrange our wedding for a week later – that way our family would still be here. Harry had said he had no family in Ireland that would come to his wedding; his parents had passed away some years ago and the rest of his family were already living in London. I had met his two sisters and his two uncles; he would be inviting them to the wedding. Harry also asked me if I would mind having one of his sisters as bridesmaid; I did not mind but my sister Margaret would be my main bridesmaid.

That Christmas in 1965 I didn't go back home, as planning my wedding would be expensive and I had to save every penny. I got an evening job working in a restaurant in Marble Arch. I wrote to Mom to tell her the news, that I would be getting married in March and I needed my birth certificate and a letter of freedom from the parish priest. Harry and I went to see the parish priest in Kilburn where we would be getting married. As Harry had no family back in Roscommon, he asked the priest if he could get his birth certificate for him. Margaret and I would go looking for wedding dresses every Saturday, and by the end of January we had bought everything that we needed for the wedding. But Harry's papers still had not turned up.

We all had a wonderful day at my brother's wedding, and it was great spending time with the family and relatives that had come from Ireland. I was sad that very few of them would be returning for my big day though. My new sister-in-law was very nice and promised that when they got back from their honeymoon, she would help me with my wedding. Hannah was very good at that sort of thing and I was glad of her help. We spoke to Father Hacked, the priest that was to marry us. He said the parish priest in Ireland was not able to help, and we would have to postpone the wedding.

The wedding plans were all put on hold. We were disappointed. I realised that my family members that were coming over for Chris's wedding, would have gone back, and it was unlikely that they would return for my wedding two months later.

It was on 14 May 1966 that our big day finally arrived, and we were married in the Sacred Heart Church, Quex Road, Kilburn. It should have been the happiest day of my life, but for some reason I was nervous. The days leading up to the wedding I was fine, excited and happy, but for some reason that morning as I was getting ready I felt different. I told myself that Harry loved me and I him, so there was no reason for me to feel that way, we would have a wonderful life together. I was nearly two months pregnant and thought maybe that was why I felt so uneasy. After the ceremony we had a reception in the Black Lion pub; it was really nice and everyone was having a good time. Harry and I were happy and my nerves had faded.

Joe Flynn was our chauffer for the day. During the evening he said to me, "You don't remember me, do you? I'm the fellow that rescued you from Hells Angels two years ago; you were a timid little creature then as I remember.' I did remember, and said, 'Thank you for that, Joe.' 'I see you did not take my advice,' he said, and went on to say, 'Harry is not a bad lad. I am sure he will look after you, and you will both be very happy.'

We didn't go on honeymoon; we had just a few days off work. We moved into a room in Cedar Road, Cricklewood, and that's where we started our married life together. Harry took me shopping for food and other things we needed for our home.

Within a week we had our first argument. I wanted to go back to see Margaret at St Cuthbert's Road, and collect some clothes for work. It wasn't too far away. Chris had also moved out of the house, and thinking Margaret would be lonely, I thought it would be better to go on my own, but Harry had other ideas and said, 'I am coming with you and we will clear out all your things. I'm not having you hopping back and forth to St Cuthbert's Road when you see fit. You are a married woman now and you are my wife. You must realise that your life will be different from now on.' I argued and tried to explain my reason, realising that it wasn't just for my sister Margaret's sake, it was also for me: I did not want to cut all ties with what had been my home for five years - after all Aggie and Johnny had been like second parents to us.

I loved Harry but did not understand his attitude. I thought it's got nothing to do with him, whether I collected my clothes or not. For the first time I felt like I was something he had bought, and wanted complete control of. I was not happy but thinking he loved me and didn't want me out of his sight, I went along with what he wanted.

Two months after we moved into Cedar Road, I decided to tell the landlady that I was pregnant, thinking that she would notice soon anyway. I did not expect the reaction that I got from her. She said, 'We can't have a baby in this house; you and your husband will have to find somewhere else to live.'

Harry soon found us a room in Kilburn. It was a big room and we shared the kitchen with two other couples. The people who owned the house were nice, always making our visitors welcome, which was usually my brother Chris and his wife Hannah, or my sister Margaret. The landlady knew I was pregnant and would often knock on our door to check that I was OK. Harry did not spend much time in the house with me. He would come home from work, have his dinner, change his clothes and would be off out again. I'd ask where he was going. He would say, just out for a drink with my mate, I won't be late, but I found he would often be very late. I did not want to sit in every night on my own and said, 'I want to go out with you.' Sometimes he would agree, and say the two of us will go out somewhere at the weekend, maybe the pictures or somewhere. But when the weekend came I did not get to go out. Harry said, 'You are pregnant, you should not be going out. Stay in and rest.' I argued that I was able to go to work, so why shouldn't I go out at the weekend at least. He said, 'I'm not arguing with you; you're not going out with me and that's final.' I was upset that he did not want to spend time with me - after all we had only been married a short time and already I felt like a prisoner.

Chapter 6

It was in early August 1966 that my younger brother Sean arrived from Ireland. He had not been able to find any decent work at home, and as Dad and he did not get on, he decided to join us in London. I was delighted to have him around. He got himself a room and a job, and he would often call to see us in the evenings. I told Sean that Harry was going out most nights, and leaving me in on my own, and that I wasn't allowed out on the weekends. Sean wasn't happy with what I had told him and said, 'Ellen you are coming out with me next Saturday night. I will pick you up at 8.30pm; you can show me around the Galtymore – that is a place I haven't been to yet.'

When Saturday arrived I was happy; I had been looking forward to going out with Sean. I had not said anything to Harry – I was not sure how to tell him, knowing full well he would disapprove, and we would have another argument. I had made up my mind that this time he would not get his own way: I was going out with my brother, no matter what he said.

That evening I was looking through the wardrobe to see what I would wear. Most of my clothes still fitted, though I was four and a half months pregnant. Harry saw me looking through the wardrobe, and said, 'Why are you changing your clothes?' I said, 'I am going out tonight; I'm fed up of being inside all the time.' He said, 'I can't take you out with me tonight. I'm going out for a drink with a couple of mates, you would not enjoy it. We will go out together next weekend.' I said, 'Harry, I have heard all this before; you always promise to take me out with you, but I have not been outside the door for months. Anyway I wasn't asking

you to take me out tonight, I'm going out with Sean.' I could see
the disapproving look on his face as he said, 'You're my wife, not
Sean's, and if anyone is going to take you out it will be me, but not
tonight.'

Sean arrived as he had promised, and after the usual greetings
to both of us, he said, 'Ellen are you not ready yet?' 'She's not
ready because she's not going out to the Galtymore with you,'
Harry said. 'She's pregnant and I'm not having her getting pushed
around in that Dance Hall in her condition.' Sean told him, 'I
know she is pregnant and I wouldn't have noticed, had she not told
me. For God's sake, Harry, there is no reason why she can't come
out with me, and if you were any kind of husband you would be
taking her out with you. Ellen told me that you go out most nights
and leave her on her own.'

Sean was really angry and said, 'What kind of a husband are
you? Ellen is twenty years old, and she should be going out and
enjoying herself, like you have been.' I did not want this dispute
to go any further, and said to Harry, 'I am going out with Sean
tonight so stop trying to make out you are protecting me.' With
that Harry said, Ok, then I am coming with you.'

We went for a drink and then on to the Galtymore. I could
sense the tension and knew Harry wasn't there to enjoy himself.
Though we had a couple of dances, it wasn't the same as when I
was his girlfriend. I was now his wife and I knew he did not want
me there with him. Saddened and disappointed that my night
out wasn't what I had hoped for, I was trying to make sense of
his attitude. Married life wasn't what I had expected; he showed
me no affection anymore. I used to think of us cuddled up on the
sofa in front of the telly every evening and going out together on
weekends, just like we used to, but my dreams and expectations

were dwindling away and I did not know what to do to make things better. Having tried talking to Harry, and telling him how I felt, he would just say I was being silly. 'You are my wife and I love you,' he would say, 'but surely a man is entitled to a drink, after a hard day's work.' I did not mind Harry going to the pub on his way home, but he usually stayed until closing time, and that was what I did not like.

It was around the end of August that the landlord knocked on our room door one evening. After inviting him in, he said, 'I'm sorry Ellen to have to tell you, we will be needing this room ourselves so you will have to move out as soon as possible.' I was shocked and knew it wasn't easy to find another place to live, especially as I was pregnant and at this stage it was getting more difficult to hide the fact. I was once again looking at shop windows for rooms to rent. I was still working so we would go out in the evenings. Most of the adverts would say no children and no pets.

One of the girls where I worked told me she had just moved out of a place in Fordwych Road. It was a room and a kitchen, and the use of the garden; it was near Kilburn Station. It sounded ideal. Giving me the address, she suggested I go and see the landlord after work. I was so pleased when the landlord said we could move in straight away. The room was quite small with a sofa bed, but it had a large kitchen, which backed on to the garden. This would be our third move in a few months and I hoped it would be our last for the foreseeable future. Harry stayed in most evenings during our first week in Fordwych Road. I was happy and thought he might settle down and in a few months we would have a baby. I was really looking forward to having the baby, and started making plans, buying an item of clothing each week. But Harry had not been giving me any money lately, and I was finding it difficult to manage on my wages. Harry had left his job and did not seem to be in any hurry to find another, so any money I had saved for the baby soon went as did the cosy nights in together.

Tom Moran, a friend of ours, would often call in the evenings. Tom would never have a full time job, even though he was a very clever man, and could turn his hand to any DIY. He was a chippy, plumber, electrician, all rolled into one. He was very well liked around Cricklewood, and everyone knew him as Baldy Tom. He soon noticed that Harry wasn't home most evenings and would say, 'Ellen where is that husband of yours? He is up to no good; he should be here with you, especially in your condition.'

It was late September and getting cold in the evenings. There was no heating in the room. We did have a small electric fire, when we moved in, but the landlord had taken it saying we were using too much electric. Sometimes I would put on the cooker in the kitchen to warm myself. Harry had got himself a job driving a lorry, and I had hoped that now he would give me some money to pay the bills, but he was not offering any, and when I asked him he would just say, 'Ellen you're working, what are you doing with your wages? I owe a few friends money and I want to pay them back.' He did not seem to understand that my wages were not enough to pay for everything but he seemed to have money to go out every night. I knew he did not care about me.

It was about this time that I first suspected that Harry was not just meeting his mates for a drink - I had a suspicion that he was seeing another woman. I did not want to believe it, but I knew something was not right. I found myself checking his clothes, going through his pockets, watching him getting ready to go out, and he wasn't sparing his Old-Spice aftershave. I knew he wasn't

32

doing all that to go out with his mates, but I still loved him and didn't want to believe what was very obvious. I wanted to talk to him about my suspicions, but decided not to. Harry was working but never seemed to have any money – what was he doing with his wages, and who was he spending it on?

It was late September; with no heating and very little food and me six months pregnant, I knew we could not carry on like this, so when he came home from work one evening I confronted him about my suspicions, and all the other problems that he had chosen to ignore. But Harry got really cross with me, saying I was being ridiculous, and how could I think that of him, but I was not convinced. I told him how embarrassed I was when my family called and there was nothing in that I could offer them to eat. So to shut me up he agreed to give me some money each week. It wasn't very much, but it helped. I worried about what would happen when I had to stop working – would Harry provide for me? I wasn't sure.

One evening our friend Tom called and said to Harry, 'You're a hard man to find in these days, I've been wanting to talk to you about something. It's getting cold in the evenings and you have no heating.' Harry told him we had a small fire, but the landlord took it away. Next evening Tom arrived just as I got home from work, saying, 'I got thinking about that fireplace and wondered if that was a working chimney you've got there, so I thought I'd call and check it out for you.'

Tom soon discovered that we could have a real fire in the grate and he could not wait to get it going. I said, 'Tom we have not got any turf or sticks.' He replied, 'You won't get any turf in this country girl, but we can get you some coal. There is a coal yard in Cricklewood near the Galty. I'll wait until Harry gets home, and we will go and put a few bags of coal in his car.' Tom waited but Harry did not come home. It was getting dark and the coal yard would be closed. Tom was still determined to get the fire going, so, as our garden was backing on to the railway grounds, he said there was bound to be some fire wood there. He went over the garden fence and anything that would burn he threw into our garden. Coming back looking pleased with himself, he said, 'Who needs coal? This will make a lovely fire.'

I was so grateful to Tom for his caring nature - if he could help, he would. I always thought of him as a good friend. We remained pals over the years, even in later years when my husband Harry would have an affair with Tom's sister. Tom was not pleased about that and would be very upset when talking to me, but it wasn't his fault, and we remained friends, until Tom died of a heart attack in 1998.

It was October 1966 when I discovered what Harry was up to. One evening after he had been home , spruced himself up, and gone back out, again saying he was going for a drink with the boys, and as usual leaving me in on my own, as he left he kissed me and said, 'I won't be late tonight.' When he arrived back at nine that night I was surprised but happy to see him. My happiness soon turned to despair when he said he had forgotten something and had to go back out; as he left I walked to the door and waved him off; as I could not see his car I stood there for a few minutes, wondering where he had parked. When he drove past, I could see there was a woman sitting in the front seat.

Going back inside I was so upset. How could he do this to me, I thought, does he not love me, or even care what happens to me.

Chapter 7

I was living mainly on bread and butter. When I got paid on Friday, I would buy sausages and potatoes, which was my diet. And he was out spending his money on women and drinking. My whole world was falling apart. Unable to tell my family what he was doing and how badly he was treating me, I pretended everything was ok when they asked. If I told my brother Chris, he would probably kill him, and if he didn't then Sean definitely would. I still loved my husband and believed that he still loved me. Despite all that I was trying to be a good wife to him and thinking that he would soon realise that, and maybe change his attitude and settle down. I couldn't have been more wrong because for the next thirty years he didn't change at all and in fact things got much worse. By the time we parted I hated and despised him. I had now changed from being that caring wife who would cry rather than retaliate to being a resentful nasty and angry person, and I did not like the person I became.

It was late October when I first started feeling unwell; I was still working though I didn't always feel well enough to work. I knew that if I didn't go to work, it would mean less food, and we had very little as it was. I was seven months pregnant and knew that I wouldn't be able to work for much longer. My sister in law Hannah would often say to me, 'Ellen you look ill and very swollen, look at your legs. You must stop working and put your feet up and rest.' Hannah was expecting a baby about the same time as me, and she had not been working for some time. Chris would not allow me to work, she would say. Within a week of Hannah's visit, my whole world fell apart, my heart was broken.

My baby was dead, and my survival was in question.

As I came home from work that day, my brother Sean was standing at the gate waiting for me. I was pleased to see him as always; we walked into the house together. I sat on a chair as Sean said, 'I've been standing out waiting for you for ages. I will go and make us a cup of tea.' As Sean went to the kitchen I felt myself getting wet, still sitting on the chair, my coat still on, I thought 'Oh my God my water has broken, and the baby isn't due for another two months.' Glancing down at my clothes, I could see it wasn't water, it was blood; the bottom half of me was soaked in blood. I called Sean as he came in from the kitchen; he looked at me and said, 'What's wrong, Ellen? You are covered in blood.' He was as shocked as I was.

I said to him, 'Go quickly and get my friend Maureen.' She lived a few streets away at no 1 Christchurch Avenue; she and her husband Rodger already had a little girl, and she would know what to do. I told Sean to leave the front door open so Maureen could get in. She arrived within 10 minutes saying, 'God, Ellen, what has happened to you?' The blood had now reached the floor and there was a big puddle of it. I wasn't feeling so well and wondered if it was the sight of the blood, or lack of it, that was making me feel so weak. Maureen had already called the doctor, and said to me, 'Don't worry you will be ok.' Her husband Rodger arrived and helped her to take off some of my outer clothes, and pulling out the sofa bed, she said to her husband, 'If Ellen is lying down the bleeding might stop.' Rodger said, 'I will go and find something to jack up the bed, that might help.' The doctor arrived and before he examined me he rang for an ambulance, saying, 'I think we need to get you to hospital as soon as possible.' He gave me an injection and listened for the baby's heartbeat, shaking his head and saying how sorry he was as he told me that my baby was dead. I was devastated, but thought maybe he was wrong, how could he be sure?

Harry came in just as the ambulance crew were putting me on to the stretcher. I could barely see him, but he looked shocked. The doctor said, 'Your wife is haemorrhaging.' Harry just said, 'What can be wrong with her? The baby isn't due for two months,' and walked straight into the kitchen. Rodger followed him. I don't know what he said, but Harry came back and walked beside me to the ambulance, though he did not come in the ambulance with me. Giving me a kiss on the forehead, he said, 'I will see you at the hospital later.' As the ambulance drove away from no 17 Fordwych Road that evening my heart was broken. I worried about my baby, was the doctor right about what he said; I wished my sister Margaret or one of my family was with me, and not realising how seriously ill I was myself, I hoped the baby would be alive.

The ambulance crew were very kind to me, reassuring me. The lady kept checking for the baby's heartbeat; I knew by the look on her face that things were not good, and as she changed my pad once again, she said, 'We have to concentrate on you now. You're still bleeding and that's not good. Your baby has passed away, I'm so sorry.' I was very upset and didn't care anymore, my baby was dead, what had I got to live for, my life was a mess. I was feeling tired and weak and just wanted to go to sleep. The ambulance had its blue lights flashing, I could see them, and thought, what is the hurry now. They were telling me we will soon be at the hospital, don't worry, you will be fine.

It was the City of London Hospital in Islington. I remember arriving at the hospital, but not being taken in. The next time I woke up I was in a room, with lots of people around me; they were talking but their voices seemed so far away. A doctor was saying, 'We've got to get the baby out now, and a C section, it's not an option, she has lost too much blood already.' I don't remember anything else about the birth of my baby. I remember thinking about my mom: she was standing at our front door back home, and she was crying. Mom always cried when any of us were leaving. She would have her bottle of Holy Water, sprinkling it on us, saying God protect us on our journey back to London. I thought a lot about my mom those first few days in hospital. If I died Margaret and Chris would have to tell her, she would cry and be so upset, knowing how I was feeling. I did not want to die; I couldn't break my mom's heart as well.

I never got to see or hold my baby son, and that broke my heart. Harry told me he was buried in Finchley but never told me exactly where; there isn't a day that goes by that I don't think about him. I spent three weeks in hospital and thought the blood transfusions would never end. Harry would come to see me every other day, sometimes bringing Margaret with him. I cried continuously and as my health improved, the more upset I became. On one of Harry's visits, he said to me, 'It's a shame you lost our baby - you could not even do that right.' How could he be so cruel?

The doctors and nurses were very kind to me, but especially matron; she would often come into the room, and sit with me. She would tell me about other patients who had lost their babies, and were coping with their loss. She was telling me about one lady who lost her baby and her husband in a short space of time. 'You are young, you have plenty of time to have children, you have a loving husband, so you must stop all this crying, it's not helping you recover,' and she told me that the doctors were pleased with my progress. 'You were very ill when you came in here. You tell me what is upsetting you so much.' I asked her if my baby had been baptised. She said, 'Yes, I made sure of that.' The matron went away, saying, 'Get some rest, and I will be back later.' She did come back later with a basin of water and a hair brush. 'Now then,' she said, 'let's tidy you up, and wash away those tears, and brush your hair. Your husband will be in later, and we can't have you looking like that. I am going off duty now but I will be in to see you in the morning. Let's hope your husband can cheer you up; he'll be pleased to see you looking more like your old self.'

On the day I was discharged from hospital my doctor told me the reason why I lost my baby was a result of blood pressure and toxaemia. 'I'm sorry to tell you that it's unlikely that you will get pregnant in the future,' he said. Hearing that did not bother me at the time. I had no plans to replace the son that I had lost. Harry wasn't happy though and questioned the doctor. 'When your son was born,' explained the doctor, 'there were complications.' I had mixed feelings about leaving hospital – at least I was safe there – and I wondered how I would feel back in Fordwych Road.

I went back to my job and everything was good. We were like a real married couple. I started to feel comfortable and confident again. Harry was working, so I was able to save some money. Harry suggested that we go home to Cork for Christmas. I was pleased; it would be our first Christmas together, and I knew Mom and Dad would be pleased to see us. Harry and I were happy in each other's company for a few months; we would go food shopping on Saturdays and for the first time since we moved into the flat there was plenty of food in the fridge and I was able to cook a proper dinner for us every evening. On one of our nights out, and after Harry had a few drinks, he said, 'Ellen, I'm so sorry. I have not been looking after you very well, but I've changed.

From now on you will come first.' Harry was a good looking man and could be quite charming, but the charm rarely surfaced, and he never apologised for anything. I thought to myself, I've been to hell and back, but at least he's said sorry, and I knew that if my brother Sean hadn't been at the house that evening I would have died – there was nobody in the house to call on, and I was afraid to get up from the chair, to go outside to get help. I never talked to Sean about that day or thanked him for saving my life, or indeed my friend Maureen or her husband Rodger who helped me all those years ago. I will be eternally grateful to them.

Harry and I moved out of Fordwych Road in June 1967 after he and his friend Mick Glynn had a dispute with the landlord over some work he had paid them to do. They had spent the money and did not finish the work. We got a room in 35 Richborough Road, off Cricklewood Broadway. Harry was back to his old habits, drinking and women, and when he was drunk he could be a right nasty person. On one occasion when I asked him to leave he said, 'Maybe I will, sure you are no good to me now; you can't have any children, so maybe I'll find a woman who can.' Harry would always pick on any imperfections a person might have, and use it.

In July 1967 I found myself back in hospital. This time I hadn't been feeling well all day, with really bad pains low in my stomach. I was on the bus coming home from work and felt I was going to be sick. So as not to get sick on the bus I got off and walked to the doctor's. He examined me, and after asking me a few personal questions, he said, 'I am sending you straight to hospital; you have got a nasty infection.' I had never heard of this and didn't know what he was talking about. In the hospital I handed over the letter my doctor gave me. After being examined again and having a blood test, a lady doctor came to see me. 'I need to ask you a few personal questions,' she said, 'I hope you don't mind.' She was asking me about my sex life, and did I have sex with any other men apart from my husband. I was very embarrassed and told her no. 'In that case you must get your husband to go and see his doctor, and you must not have sex with him while he is being treated. I am giving you some medication you must take, and go and see your own doctor in 10 days.'

I confronted Harry telling him what the doctor had said. He said, 'There is nothing wrong with me; you must have picked it up from a dirty toilet somewhere.' I did not believe him and made him keep his distance. I found out later that he had been treated in hospital before I became ill. He had already infected me. I often wonder why it was that I didn't leave him. I could have walked away but I didn't. I guess it was my strict Catholic upbringing, afraid of God's punishment, till death do us part and all that, so I felt I had to stick with it, for better, for worse - and in my mind it couldn't get much worse.

Chapter 8

In November of that year, I missed a period, and remembering that I could not have children I thought well I am not pregnant. When nothing happened in December I was worried and thought what else can go wrong with me, and as we had planned to go home for Christmas I felt I should see the doctor. I had great news that day. The doctor told me I was two months pregnant. 'I will arrange for you to have more tests, to confirm it, so don't get too excited yet.' All the tests were positive. I was delighted. I told Harry my news; he was pleased but not over excited. The rest of my family were happy for me. Dad threw his cap in the air, and said, 'Them doctors are not always right.'

On 3 July 1968 we had a beautiful baby girl. She was born in Queen Mary's Maternity Hospital in Hampstead and we called her Katie Philomena. I could not take my eyes off her, and could not believe she was mine. Harry was a great help to me in the beginning, but the novelty of having a baby to look after soon wore off. I loved taking her out in her pram, and showing her off to my friends.

The room we lived in was too small for us. Harry said he would look for a flat; we needed more room, now that we had a baby. It was hard to manage on the money Harry was giving me, and if we got a flat, it would be more expensive, so I needed to get a part time job. I looked through the local paper. There was a vacancy for a cleaner in a pub in Kilburn. It was the North London public house. It was for three hours every morning. After speaking to the pub landlord, I asked him if I could take a baby with me, telling him she would be in her pram. I got the job. It was not one of my favourite jobs, but I needed the money. Having to clean both bars and toilets was hard work, especially at weekends. I often had to clean shit, piss and vomit; sometimes it would be so bad that I would get sick myself. I consoled myself with the fact that I had a lovely baby daughter, and thinking that my stomach would get used to this cleaning lark, and it wouldn't seem so bad. It was a job, and the money was useful.

We moved into a flat in 21 Ash Grove in Cricklewood in January 1969. It was a two bedroom, on the second floor, with our own sitting room and kitchen, bathroom and toilet. So much space, it was wonderful. My sister Margaret offered to rent one of the bedrooms to help us. Having her with us was an added bonus. By this time Margaret knew what Harry was like, and had no respect for him. If he was in Margaret would stay in her room. Having friends living in the same street was great. Jack was the local barber and a really nice person. He was Greek and his wife Sadie came from Tipperary. They always made me so welcome; they were great people and I had a lot of respect for them.

On one of my visits to their house, Sadie said, 'Ellen, I feel there is something you should know. I hate to see that man making a fool of you, but he is going out with Tom's sister Patricia, and it's been going on for some time. I'm so sorry.' My heart sank. I knew it was true. Jack and Sadie wouldn't have told me unless they were certain. That evening I confronted him but as usual he denied it, saying, 'Ellen do you believe everything you hear?' and, 'It's rubbish.' I did not want to believe it, but in my heart I knew it was true. It was around that time that I suspected that I might be pregnant again. Katie was only eight months old. I told Harry. He seemed shocked but said, 'Don't worry, we will manage. I suppose that means that you will be looking for more money off me.'

Margaret and I had bought a few things for the flat; it was looking nice and very comfortable. We had bought a record player, some records of the Beatles, the Bee-Gees and I already had some Irish records and would spend hours listening to them; I loved my records. It made me feel that I was still in touch with the outside world, as I never got out socially, much as I would have loved to.

One night as I got ready for bed, it was late. Looking out of the bedroom window, to my shock and horror, Harry and Patricia were sitting in her car right under our bedroom window. I was thinking why couldn't they park around the corner or in another street – it was like they wanted me to see them. I wanted to go outside and kill both of them. I was so angry; how they could be so cruel?

I went to bed thinking I can't have a row with him tonight. Katie was asleep in her cot and my sister was next door. And not wanting to wake them up I pretended to be asleep when he came in. He did eventually come in and into bed. Adding insult to injury and after trying to wake me up, he started to perform, and when I said, 'No leave me alone,' he raped me. Lying there with tears rolling into my ears I thought I hate this man. I wished he would die. I thought what have I done, I have married a monster. In the sixties and seventies domestic violence was rarely heard of, or most people wouldn't report it. The police would rarely interfere, and if it was your husband, violence seemed to be acceptable. So like a lot of other women in similar situations, I had to accept my fate, as it was. My husband was a controlling bully. He obviously did not care who he hurt; everything he did was for his own satisfaction and it didn't matter who he stamped on to get what he wanted.

Chapter 9

My Son Steven was born on 28 November 1969 in St Mary's Hospital, Harrow Road. He was a lovely blond blue eyed baby, and again I was a very proud mom. His dad came to visit a few times but it was mainly my brother Chris who would visit. His wife Hannah was looking after Katie for me. Back then mothers and their babies would be in hospital for at least one week, and someone would have to come to the hospital to collect them when they were being discharged. A nurse would escort them to the front entrance. Harry had not been in the hospital for a few days, and I had no way of getting in touch with him, to collect me.

The doctor had said in the morning that my baby and I could go home. I waited all day in the hope that someone would turn up. It was late afternoon and I was getting desperate. I rang Joe Flynn. His was the only phone number I knew, as Harry worked for him at the time, and I hoped he might know where Harry was. I told Joe, 'I'm Harry's wife, and I need him to collect me and my son from the hospital.' He said, 'Where is that good for nothing husband of yours? He should be collecting his wife and son. I will see if I can track him down. I'll make sure someone is there to collect you within the hour.'

Ringing Joe was embarrassing and humiliating for me. I did not want Joe and his wife Margaret talking about me. They all knew Harry, and what he was like; they would have known the girl he was going out with, as she lived on the same street. Joe was known as a hard man around Cricklewood. He was one of the Sunshine Gang. He would not take any nonsense from anybody. That day when he said he would track Harry down to pick me up from hospital, I worried that Harry would be mad at me for ringing Joe, and what if he got cheeky with Joe. I did not want any trouble. Harry deserved a good kicking, and at that time I wished someone would do just that. But he was my husband and I had to be loyal to him. There were people who would speak badly about the Sunshine Gang. I judge people as I find them and those men who had run-ins with Joe, if any of them were anything like my husband, then I would say they deserved what they got.

Life back in 21 Ash Grove didn't get any easier; with two small children to look after, I was kept busy. They were more important than anything else. Money was scarce now that I was not working, and I could not rely on Harry. At least he was paying the rent on the flat - or so he said; all I would have to find money for was food and clothes for the children. With the rent Margaret was giving me and the children's allowance we managed. We had been living in the flat for just over one year. There were letters coming for Harry. I would never open his mail; I was not allowed to. He would always open his letters in private, and never left them on display.

When the bailiffs knocked on the door that first week in March, I did not know what to do. Harry was out and Margaret had left for work. The bailiffs were telling me the rent had not been paid in months. And they had a court order for our eviction. 'You have been given plenty of notice,' they were telling me. 'We will be back in seven days, and we will be taking possession of this flat.'

I was in a state of shock; I had no idea the rent was not being paid. I knew then what the letters Harry had been getting were about. Had he told me I would have got the money from one of my family, and now it was too late. This is my home and everything we put into it will be gone in a week. Telling Margaret that evening really upset me - after all it was her home too. She said, 'Don't worry about me, I can easily find a room, but Ellen what about you and the two children? You won't be able to find a place that easy, and not in one week.'

My brother Sean had visited us a few weeks previously. He was now working out of London, and we did not see him very often. I had no way of getting in touch with him, so he couldn't help. When Harry came home that evening both Margaret and I were waiting for him. Margaret was saying, 'What the hell are you playing at? You did not have the decency to tell us you were not paying the rent.' I told him about the bailiffs and that we were going to be evicted next week. 'Calm down,' he said, 'I will find us another flat,' as if it was no big deal. 'I will have everything out of here before they come back. Give me a couple of days.' Margaret was very angry, saying why didn't he tell us. Harry told her, 'I said I would deal with it, didn't I? What do you think, that I'd have my wife and two children thrown out on the street?'

That is exactly what he did do. Within a few days Margaret had found a room, and had moved. Harry was reassuring me that everything would be OK. He had found a place close by. 'I just need to finalise a few things with the estate agent,' he said. Packing our things into boxes, and getting things ready to move, was very sad for me. I had loved this flat and had made it my home. We had only two days left, and I was getting worried. Was Harry lying to me? Did he really have some place else for us to go? The bailiffs would be here on Friday - it was now Thursday. Harry had gone out that morning; he had not come back. I waited and worried, but he never came home.

Next day the bailiffs were at the door at 10am. They could see I was upset, and asked where my husband was. After telling them I did not know, they said, 'Where is all this stuff going? We can give you one hour to get yourself sorted. Just take the things you want for now. Your husband can make arrangements to collect the rest later.'

After telling them that the children and I had no place to go, one of them said, 'That's not really our problem.' His companion was more considerate and said, 'Don't worry I will get in touch with Social Services; I am sure they will help you.'

That morning in March 1970, as I stood on the corner of Ash Grove with my two small children, I was still hoping that my husband would turn up, and rescue us. Holding Steven in one arm and Katie standing beside me, her arms wrapped around my legs and wanting to be picked up, I felt old and useless. Not knowing where I was going, if only I had my pram I thought, at least the children would be comfortable. I wondered how long we would have to stand there. The social services were coming to pick us up. I hoped it would be soon.

My arms were aching, and the children were feeling cold and restless. Katie looked up at me saying, 'Mommy cry-baby.' That was something I would say, when baby Steven cried. Eventually a car pulled up beside us. A woman got out and said, 'You are, Mrs McGovern. My name is Mary and I'm from social services.' Helping us into her car, she said, 'Sorry I am a bit late, you must be frozen, I am so sorry you had to wait so long. Your situation only came to our attention a couple of hours ago. I need to take some details from you, your full name, date of birth, and also the children's.'

After she had finished writing, she asked, 'Where is your husband?' I told her I did not know. 'Oh,' she said, 'so it's just you and the two children. Have you any family that can help?' I told her, 'No, most of my family live in Ireland.' 'You have two lovely children,' she said, 'and I can see they have been well looked after, up to now. But under the circumstances I think it would be best for the children if I arranged for them to be taken into care.'

Was I hearing right, I thought, could this woman forcibly take my children, what is she talking about? I told her, 'You are not taking my children,' as I went to open the car door. 'We'll manage,' I said, 'thank you.' I was not thinking at the time where we would go, but wherever it would be, we were staying together. She put her arm back to stop me getting out of the car. 'I am sorry Mrs McGovern,' she said, 'it was only a suggestion, I thought it might help you, give you a chance to get yourself sorted out. You have two very small children there, will you be able to cope on your own, with no husband or family support?' I told her, 'We will be fine, all I need is a place to live.'

'I am sorry if I upset you,' she said. 'It's my fault, I should have explained myself better. Don't worry,' she said, 'now that I understand what you want, I will take you to Finchley. You'll be comfortable there. It's a nice little flat, it's four pounds a week,' she said, 'can you manage that?' I told her I had very little money. 'Don't worry,' she said, 'I will stop off in Regents Park Road, that's where the benefit office is, and as your husband's not with you, you will be entitled to some benefit.' I didn't know what she was talking about. What was this Benefit? I had never heard of it. I was desperate and any help they would give me would be appreciated.

That afternoon Mary dropped us off at the flat. It was called the coach house. It wasn't far from Woodside Park station. I did not know the area and felt a bit lost. Cricklewood, and my family and friends seemed a long way off. Before Mary left she said, 'You'll find shops at Tally-Ho, it is not too far,' pointing in the direction. After unpacking my case, I set about feeding the children. They were hungry and tired after the day. That's when I realised I had no food for myself. I'd have loved a cup of tea. But without milk or tea it wasn't possible. I did not sleep much that night. As it was in a flat over a garage, and not in a house, I felt unsafe. Being on my own, with two small children was daunting.

Next morning I was really hungry and knew I would have to go out and find these shops. I also knew that taking Katie and Steven with me wasn't going to be easy. Katie was only 20 months and Steven wasn't yet four months old. I would have to carry both of them most of the way. If only I had a pushchair, I thought. I could only buy a few items. So I chose bread, butter, milk and tea. I had also phoned my friend Sadie to tell her where I was. Sadie would let Margaret know, and I felt sure she would come to visit. I spent the first couple of days looking out of the window hoping to see a familiar face, and eventually I did see a familiar face. It was my sister Margaret. I could not have been more delighted. She had bought me cakes and biscuits and for a couple of hours I had an adult to talk to.

Margaret suggested I go and get a few days' shopping and she would look after the children. 'Make sure you get everything you need,' she said. 'I will be back by the time you need anything else. You can't be carrying two small children with you and shopping as well.'

In the next six months I was moved three times. The next one was in Edgware. It was a huge building with communal kitchens, and washrooms. I did not like the place; it was very dirty. I could see that the children living in the next room had nits in their hair. They were much older than my children and would often play on the landing. Sometimes they would knock, and ask if they could take Katie out to play. I always made some excuse to them. Katie had long blond hair, and I could not risk her catching their nits.

The rooms were big and sometimes they would put two families in one room. I had been there three weeks when the caretaker came and said, 'I have another family who will be sharing your room. It's a mother and her two boys. The boys are five and seven. They would be company for you.' They were company, and we seemed to get on ok but unfortunately within the first couple of weeks she started sneaking her boyfriend in, keeping him overnight. The rule of the house was that all visitors were to be out by 11pm but she allowed him to stay all night, and this was becoming a regular thing, and he stayed most nights. She had not asked me if I minded. I did not feel confident enough to tell her that I did mind. My bed was just inside the front window, with Katie's cot across the foot of the bed. I felt that it was safer for Katie to sleep in the cot, and Steven in the bed with me.

The other woman and her two boys slept in the opposite side of the room, the boys in a single bed and their mother next to them in a double. She would sometimes go out at night and I would take care of her boys. I enjoyed looking after them; they were good kids.

One night I woke to find her boyfriend standing at the window, which was beside my bed and Katie's cot. He was looking out of the window, smoking, dressed only in his underpants. This was my side of the room; I felt I should tell them. He shouldn't stand there smoking by my daughter's cot. Next morning I politely told her how I felt. She said, 'Sorry, I will have a word with him.' I did not like sharing the room with those people. I wanted to tell the caretaker what was happening but felt that would be mean. Some weeks later I glanced at Katie's cot one morning to find she was not there. She would usually be standing up in her cot at this time; as I looked around she was lying on the floor. The two boys were with her, they were taking off her nappy. 'What are you doing?' I said. 'And why have you taken Katie from her cot?' The oldest boy said, 'Ellen, she was wet, and we were only trying to change her nappy.' Their mother was still sleeping so I told them to go back to bed. I was not happy and wondered if there was more to it than they were saying. She was a little girl - were they just being inquisitive? Their mother was sleeping with her boyfriend a few feet away from them. I was worried about my daughter's safety. I felt I had no choice, but to tell the caretaker.

To my surprise she said, 'We have known for some time about her boyfriend; she is on her last warning. We have been making arrangements to have the family moved.' Needless to say I was pleased and for the rest of the time I spent in that half-way house, it was my two children and I that occupied that room. I found myself a job cleaning a shop every morning, and with the help of a pushchair that the caretaker had given me, I was able to take Katie and Steven with me. Having the pushchair also meant I could get back to visit my friend in Cricklewood.

My brother Chris and his family were living in Westbourne Park, so I could also visit them. They also had two children. Hannah and I would often walk around Portobello Road market - that was a real treat for me. Chris and Hannah's flat wasn't huge but she would often invite us to stay overnight, which we did on one occasion.

The rules of the house in Edgware were strict: we had to stay there every night, and be in by ten o'clock. I felt like a prisoner. I was 24 years old and now a single parent. Often as I was on the bus on the way back to the home, I would see all the people queuing to get into the Galtymore club, and would so wish that I was one of them.

I had not seen Harry since I was evicted from 21 Ash Grove Road; it was obvious he hadn't any interest in us. Sometimes I would ask Margaret if she had seen him. She would hesitate, and tell me, 'Ellen, forget about him.' 'But I want to know,' I would say. She would tell me, 'I have seen him around a few times, he is still with the same woman.' News like this didn't upset me anymore, I told Margaret, so don't let it worry you.

Chapter 10

It was August and yet again I was being moved, to a new building, a one bedroom self-contained flat. I had my own front door with no restrictions. The caretaker said, 'You will soon be offered your own place.' I would have gladly stayed where I was. It was clean, bright and all the furniture was new. This new place was in Burnt Oak, and near the shops. So every day we would go out and walk around the stores; not having much money I did not buy very much. But I did a lot of window shopping. I would sometimes walk back to Cricklewood along the Edgware Road; I enjoyed walking and looking at the shops. I especially enjoyed checking out the car showrooms, and dreaming of a time when I would have my own car. I knew it would not be anytime soon, but things would eventually get better for me. First I had to get my own home, then a good job, then I could start saving for my car.

Making all these plans as I walked made me feel great. I would tell myself that one day everything will come good. I will be independent and won't need help from anybody, especially my husband; I already knew what he was like in the helpful department. I would often talk to my daughter Katie as we walked along. I would tell her about my plans. She would not say much, and often looked at me as if I was mad, but she'd smile and I knew she understood. She wasn't even two years old, but she was the only one I had to talk to at that time.

I never lost sight of my dream of a better life, and though nothing had gone right for me in the past, I hoped things would improve in the future. Things did eventually come good for me, but in the meantime, I would endure a lot more heartache and hardship, some of which was my own fault. I let my heart rule my head and that had always been my downfall.

In September 1970 I had a letter from Barnet Council offering me a permanent home in Cricklewood. It was a two bedroom house; I was so pleased I could not wait to see it. Though I had lived in the area before I had no idea where this place was. Next morning I put the children in the pushchair and set off for Cricklewood, thinking somebody there will direct me to this address. The house was fifteen minutes' walk from Cricklewood Broadway. I had a back and front garden. I could not have been more pleased, and I felt like I was coming home – I would be near my family and friends.

I had made arrangements to go to the council to collect my keys and sign the necessary paper work. I would be moving in one week's time. I was really excited. I could see that the house had not been lived in for some time – the garden was overgrown with briers and nettles; the house was totally empty. I don't know what I expected, but suddenly I realised we had no furniture, no cooker or fridge, not even a bed, just bare floorboards. I thought if only I had an electric kettle I could make the baby's milk and heat Katie's tins of food.

As I stood at the back door, the lady that lived in the house at the back called me. I made my way down the garden, through the nettles to introduce myself to her. She said, 'My name is Lily. I notice you have two small children with you, have you just moved in?' She went on to say, 'If I can help you in any way, I will be glad to.' I said, 'If you wouldn't mind giving me some boiling water, it would be a great help. I haven't got a kettle.' 'I have a spare one that you can have, and you can put it on the gas cooker.' 'Thank you,' I said, 'but I don't have a cooker.' 'Oh,' she said, 'in that case, give me a shout any time, and I will boil some water for you.'

Later that day Lily knocked on the front door. She handed me her electric kettle saying, 'I'm sorry, I didn't think. Sure I can use my cooker to boil water, and you can use this one.' I felt I should invite her in, though I was a little embarrassed that she would see we had no furniture. She was a kind lady so I invited her in. As she walked inside, she looked shocked, and said, 'Oh my goodness, Ellen, you have no furniture. When is it being delivered?' Thinking that there was no point in lying to her, I said, 'I don't have anything to be delivered.' She seemed concerned. She said, 'You do have a bed, don't you?' As I shook my head, she said, 'Where are you and your children going to sleep tonight? I told her we would be OK. 'I have a couple of blankets; we can make a bed on the floor.' 'I have spare bedding,' she said. 'I will go and get it.' I thought after she had gone, what a kind and generous person. I am a stranger to her and she can't do enough to help me – why can't everyone be like her? She reminded me of my mother.

I had already applied to the Council for a grant, to help me furnish the house, and I thought, when that comes, I will be able to buy a cooker and bed first. If there is any money left I can buy lino for the floor. Over the next few months I gradually got bits of furniture and other things that we needed. I never managed to get my belongings that I had to leave behind at 21 Ash Grove, but with the help of my sister Margaret and brother Chris my new home was nearly complete.

Looking around my new home and my two beautiful children, I made a promise to myself that nobody would ever make me leave my home again. In the past four years I had moved nine times and this was to be the last. Living at no 94 was great, both for me and the children. We were happy there most of the time. Katie made some new friends – two little girls, who lived a few doors away; they were much older than Katie, but would often come in to play with her. The girls noticed that there was no man in the house. They would say to Katie, 'You have not got a dad. We've got a dad, where is your dad?' Katie would get upset saying, 'I want my daddy.' She was too young to understand, so I would tell her your daddy will be back soon. He is working away.

My friend Tom Moran came to tidy up the garden, and do some other jobs, like hanging curtains. Tom was always a great help to us. He would never charge any money for his help, which was appreciated very much. There were not many people like Tom; usually there would be a price to pay but with Tom that was not the case. He was just kind and if he could help somebody he would.

The first year, in my new home, was the happiest I'd been for a long time. It was so peaceful, I felt completely in control, and I realised that everything was better since Harry was not around; I nearly forgot that I was married.

A new family had moved into the house across the road: Tony and Debbie, they had four young boys and at the time the two youngest, Peter and Michael, were the same age as my children. The two older boys Tommy and Peter had just started school. Tony was a Galway man and Debbie was from Kerry. They were really nice people, and we became great friends. It was great having such a nice family across the road. Having them made me feel safe; if I had a problem I could always rely on them to help. We were always borrowing things from each other. It could be a cup of sugar, milk or potatoes – that's the way it was. Her children would be in my house, or mine in hers. And we always knew they were safe.

Chapter 11

My husband Harry had found where we lived and one day there was a knock on the door, and there he was, large as life. 'Are you going to invite me in?' he said. 'How are you and the kids?' he asked. Katie remembered him, and was pleased to see her daddy. But Steven did not know who he was and would not go near him. He had a good look around the house, saying, 'This is a nice place, you're so lucky to get a house. This will be good for us and our family, and I missed you so much.' I said, 'Harry, there is no us anymore. Remember you left us in the street outside 21 Ash Grove with no home or no money, when the bailiffs put us out. We needed you then but you just left us.' After spending some time talking to Katie, and trying to win Steven's attention, he left. I knew I could never trust Harry again. He had not offered any financial help or indeed any kind of help. So I thought maybe things had not worked out between him and the woman he had been seeing for the past two years, and he now wanted a home. I was not ready to forgive him, for all the hurt he had caused me, and I couldn't let him back into my life.

My family in Ireland did not know we were living apart. In fact they knew nothing of the hardship I had endured, since getting married. We all thought it best not to tell them. They would worry, especially Mom. She would worry about the religious aspect, as well as the fact the children were without a father. As I said before Mom was very religious, and would blame herself for allowing me to come to this country She would be on her knees 24/7 asking for God's help, and that wouldn't be fair on her.

Going home on holiday was sometimes difficult; I hated lying to my parents. When they asked why Harry wasn't with us, I would say he couldn't get the time off work. And then I made up stories about what we did and where we went socially. Having to tell them what a good man he was, a good husband and father, and provider (all untrue), I hoped and wished that one day it would all be true, and I would be proud of my husband.

Harry started to call to see the children, sometimes once a week. We might not see him for a month, but it was always about him when he did call, his right to be with his family, his right to live with his wife. He would tell me I was depriving the children of their father, and how wrong that was. He would remind me of my marriage vows, and tell me how much he loved me.

Remembering how badly he had let me down in the past, how he had betrayed me and neglected his children, I could not forgive him and thought we would be better off without him. Katie was always pleased to see her daddy when he would call. Steven was still wary of him, though the packet of smarties he would give him were helping to win him over. Steven would cling to me when his daddy was around, making it clear that it would take more than a packet of smarties to win his affection. Harry would get mad with Steven's attitude towards him, and call him a little puff and a mommy's boy. Harry would say, 'Look what you have done to the child, you're turning him into a Nancy Boy.' His comments would make me so angry and we would end up shouting at each other. Harry couldn't understand that to Steven he was a stranger. Steven was only four months old when his dad left us on the street. He was now two years old and did not know his dad. I told Harry that Steven was my son and whatever he grew up to be it was fine by me, he is my boy and I will still love him. Harry left saying, 'You are not fit to be a mother.'

As the years passed Steven and his dad never got on, even when he grew up; no matter how Steven tried to please his dad, it was never good enough. His dad would never say, well done, or good lad. Harry would never give Steven credit for anything he had done. Harry's criticism and nastiness took its toll on Steven, though I would always try to defuse the situation. Steven grew up lacking confidence and self-worth. Unlike his dad Steven had always been very soft hearted, and his dad's attitude towards him had a lasting effect on him. I would say, 'Steven, take no notice of your dad, you are a good boy and your dad is just being his usual nasty self.' Steven would say, 'Mom, why does Dad not like me, why does he always pick on me? He never says anything to the girls, and it's always me.' This wasn't true because he showed the same contempt for his daughters. Katie was very close to her dad as a child. She would say to me, 'Why can't our dad live with us? My friends down the road have their dad. Why does my daddy not stay with us?'

I was happy with my life as it was at that time, and did not want Harry around. I found a job as a waitress in Golders Green from 8pm to 1am. It was in a posh Italian restaurant, and the pay was good. I knew a girl that lived nearby, who was happy to babysit. Her family were not well off, so she was happy to earn some money. I also had a part time job every morning working in a pub, the Cricklewood Hotel. And I was able to take the children with me. It was mainly cooking breakfast for the bar staff, making beds and cleaning the rooms. The pub would be still closed so Katie and Steven could play around the bar. Mr and Mrs White were my bosses, such nice people, and very understanding. They were happy to keep an eye on the children while I did my work.

My two jobs enabled me to save some money for that car I

dreamed of buying. I was so excited at the prospect of owning my
own car. I had set myself a goal that in six months I would have
enough money saved. The fact that I did not have a driving licence
and did not know how to drive didn't seem to bother me!

Harry was still pleading with me to let him live with us,
promising that he would look after us and give me money. 'I'll
give up the drink,' he said. 'I know how stupid I have been in the
past, but I do really love you.' He would call to the house late at
night asking if he could stay. I wanted to believe him that he was
a changed man. I told him to give up the drink first, and I would
think about the future then.

My younger sister Mary had come to live in London, and was
staying with me. She was young and a bit wild; I found it hard to
keep track of her. I worried that she might meet a man that would
take advantage of her innocence. I suppose I did not want her
making the same mistakes that I had made.

My sister Margaret suggested that I should go to the Galtymore
one night with Mary, and she would look after the children. She
said, 'Ellen you have not been outside the door for about four
years. Now you have someone to go with, so just go. The children
will be fine; you have some fun for a change.'

Mary and I did go out that weekend, and had a great time.
It was a wonderful feeling being out and free for a few hours. I
thought to myself I can get out more often now, with the help
of my two sisters. On arrival home that night, the lights were
still on; it was two thirty in the morning and I wondered why
Margaret was still up. As I walked into the living room, Harry
was sitting there with Katie on his lap. He started shouting and
swearing at me calling me a whore, saying, 'You went out whoring
around the Galtymore and left your kids.' I tried to take Katie

from him; she had her hands out to me, but he would not let her go. I could see she was nervous.

Margaret told me he had called at midnight. She told him I was out and the children were in bed, but he forced his way in and refused to leave. He had gone upstairs and had taken Katie from her bed. 'I asked him to leave, but he refused, saying I need to be here to look after my children, seeing that their mother isn't looking after them; her social life seems more important to her.' I tried to reason with him saying this was the first time I had been out in nearly four years. But he would not listen.

I asked Margaret to go out to the phone box, down the road and call the police, which she did. He was still swearing and calling me names. 'You called the police,' he said. 'No fucking police are going to put me out of here.' When the police came Harry told them that I had gone out and left the kids on their own, and it was lucky he had called. I told them that wasn't true. Margaret explained the situation to them, how he had knocked on the door at midnight and took Katie from her bed. The policeman said to Harry, 'Now give the little girl to her mother,' but again he refused, telling the Officer, 'She is my wife and this is my daughter, and I don't need any help from you lot.' The policeman said to him, 'Your wife called us, and I can see why now. I will take the little girl from you, and then you can leave. If you refuse we will arrest you.'

Harry was always a stubborn man and liked to get his own way. He would go out and enjoy life to the full, and thought that was his right. But for me there were different rules. He would often treat me with physical abuse, saying, 'Ellen I will put your effing head through the window, I'll make such a mess of your face that no one else will look at you. I'll teach you to be a good wife.' Usually his anger was fuelled by drink. He could be kind and very sociable when he was sober. I would try reasoning with him, when he was in a good mood asking him why he was so angry, why he treated me so badly. His response would always be the same, and it would always be my fault.

Harry was jealous of me and would hate anyone paying me any attention. He would get into a rage. It got so bad that when we went out together, I would put my head down and look the other way. If we met anyone I knew I would try to avoid speaking to them. If a man said hello to me I knew I would be in trouble. I would question my own behaviour. Was it partly my fault Harry was behaving the way he was? What could I do to make him happy? But deep down I knew it was not me. The only reason that he treated me badly was that he knew he could. He knew how to put on a show for people who might come to visit. He portrayed himself as a kind, hard-working husband and provider, telling them how hard it was to keep a wife and family. Those kids have their hands out for money, he would say, when realistically it would be him that would be looking for the hand outs. He hated to see me giving money to the children; as they got older they would need new trainers, and things for school, he would shout at them and say, 'Your mother has no money to be giving you.' He would begrudge them any money I gave them, in case there wasn't enough left for himself.

Writing this now makes me so angry at myself: how could I have been such a fool, such a pushover? Harry had no respect for me or the children, yet I tried to please him. I spent most of my life looking after him and trying to please him, and tending to all his every needs, in the hope that one day he would appreciate what he had - a loyal wife and beautiful children.

Harry continued to call to see Katie and Steven, only now he

would visit early evening and without drink. He would bring
something for the children, a little toy or something and he was
much more agreeable. He would say, 'Ellen you will never see me
taking a drink again. I've been such an idiot.' I was not convinced,
and I would tell him, 'You have the last bit right, but I have heard
all these promises before, and you could never stay sober for more
than a few days. So we will see how you get on this time.'

I knew Harry wanted to come and live with us, and at the time
I did feel sorry for him - at least now he was trying. I knew Katie
and Steven needed their father. I would see the family across the
road, and wish my family could be more like them (complete). A
united couple, a kind and loving husband and father, with four
boys that adored him. Tony also liked to go for a drink, always in
moderation; the drink never changed his character, and he would
still be the same sociable man, playing with the kids, dancing
around the living room with them, and never a cross word.

Katie was three and Steven 18 months when I finally let Harry
move back in with us. He was still off the drink and we were
happy. He had suggested I should stay at home and look after the
children. 'You don't need to work,' he said. 'I will give you enough
money. Looking after these two is a full time job.' It was good
hearing him say that; it had not been easy for me coping with
the kids and my jobs - besides, I had bought my car and did not
need to save. Finally I had everything that I wanted. I had bought
a Mini Cooper that I had seen advertised locally; it was blue in
colour. I didn't know how to drive it, but looking at it parked
outside the house made me feel very proud. I thought if I drive it a
few yards every day I will soon get the hang of it.

In the evening when the children were tucked up in bed, I'd sit
in my car driving it a few yards forward and back, going a little

further each day. Gradually I was confident enough to drive to the end of the road and back. I was feeling pleased with myself – I could now drive! I got insurance and tax, but I still had no driving licence. I was always very careful not to draw attention to myself, knowing if the police stopped me I would surely be in trouble. I loved my blue Mini Cooper and continued to drive it without a licence for the next three years. I did eventually pass my driving test, after failing at my first attempt.

Back in the seventies everyone around Cricklewood seemed to know each other, even the local bobby who would be around the Broadway seemed to know everybody's business and he often stopped me when driving; he would say to me, 'Mrs McGovern, have you got your licence yet? I'll have to report you, don't let me catch you again.' His name was Charlie and every time he stopped me, he would say the same thing: 'Don't let me catch you again.' Charlie was a friendly man and would like to stop and talk to people as he walked around the Broadway. He would spend much time in Jack the barber's; Jack's wife Sadie was a great friend of mine. I expect that's how he knew who I was and who I was married to. Harry used the same barber shop for his haircuts. Jack's barber shop was like a meeting place for some of the men, especially for the Irish lads who had no jobs, and no place else to go. That was a place they could go without spending any money, and most of them didn't have a penny to spend.

Chapter 12

It was six months now since Harry had moved into the house with us and although he would throw the odd temper tantrum things generally weren't too bad. He had gone back on the drink but in moderation – it was not every night like it used to be. I still worried that he was working his way back to his old habits. I was always on edge waiting for the night when he would come through the door drunk and out of control. I would tell myself to stop worrying about something that might never happen. Harry and I were both working and financially we had money to buy whatever we needed for the children and ourselves. Harry was never too generous with his money. He had been giving me some cash every week, but even with my wages I found it hard to save any. I had not been home to see my family for over a year and desperately wanted to see them; after all, I had allowed them to believe that Harry was a hard working generous man, so they would wonder why we hadn't been home. Mom would say in her letters, 'Ellen when are you coming home? Maybe you could come and spend Christmas with us this year? It would be great to see you and the children.'

At the time people back home were under the impression that people living and working in London had plenty of money which wasn't always the case. I never knew what poverty was as a youngster growing up in Ireland. We did not have meat and two veg every day, but we always had plenty of food; it wouldn't be the best but we were never hungry.

It wasn't until after I was married that I experienced the true meaning of poverty and what it was like to be really hungry. That was a long time ago in the late 60s or early 70s. It was a bad time for me back then, but I believe bad experiences make you stronger and more determined in life. In my next letter to Mom I made another excuse as to why I wasn't going home for Christmas, telling her we had planned to go next summer. 'I will definitely be home the end of July,' I told her.

Katie and Steven were in nursery school and soon would be in school full time, and I could get a better job; so far I had only been able to work in jobs where I could take them with me. Harry would never want to babysit. I had often talked to him about me getting a job in the evenings, but he would always dismiss the idea, saying, 'I can't be in every evening looking after the kids. They would drive me mad; you'll have to manage with what you've got.'

Harry had got to know other men around the estate where we lived, and would often bring them to the house. 'Ellen,' he would say, 'make my friend a cup of tea and a sandwich,' or if I was cooking dinner it would be, 'give this man a bit of dinner.' Harry would never ask me if there was enough to go around. On those occasions I would have to give my dinner to his friend. The loving, caring, helpful promises he had made me a year ago when he moved in to live with us were dwindling away. He was spending more time in the local pub. I worried about him losing his job, because the more he drank the less interested he was in his work, and us as a family. He was acting again as if he had no responsibility; he was a husband and father, and should be providing for us, instead of acting like a single man with not a care in the world.

When I would remind him of the promises he had made to me, he would say, 'Shut up, you are always nagging me, isn't a man entitled to go out and have a drink after a hard day's work?' I would argue with him that the children and I were not benefiting from his work as he was spending all his wages in the pub. I could argue with him forever, but nothing would sink in, he just didn't care. It was at this time I started thinking there must be some way I could stop him drinking, thinking if I could make him sick every time he came home drunk, maybe he would think the drink was not agreeing with him and give it up. He would always want tea when he got home, so I got thinking maybe putting a few drops of washing liquid in his tea would work. It didn't, so I increased the amount and hoped that he wouldn't taste it. He did not notice but he didn't get sick either. I would have to try something else.

Next time I went shopping I bought laxatives. This is bound to work I thought to myself. That evening I crushed them up, and made his favourite dinner, lamb stew, and as I watched him eat every bit, I was quite pleased with myself. Then he said, 'That was a nice bit of stew, Ellen, is there enough left for tomorrow?' I had given him double the recommended dose, and continued with this over the next few days. Not knowing if the tablets were having any effect on him and as he had not changed his routine, I soon realised that in fact I was wasting my time. Having accepted the fact that I had no control over him, and knowing that he would please himself no matter what I said, I gave up trying.

Steve and Katie were now in school so I could work longer hours, but the more I earned the more Harry spent, and though he would give me money on Friday, by Monday he would be taking it back. Telling him no was not an option, because he would keep on and on, so much so that eventually I would give in just to get rid of him.

Chapter 13

Our daughter Millie was born on 4 August 1973, though initially it was a shock to me when I found out I was pregnant. I had promised Mom and Dad that I would go home that summer, and felt that I couldn't let them down again. I had been looking forward to going home, but I knew I could not manage to take three children on that train and boat by myself. So on one of my hospital visits I asked to speak to a social worker. I had thought if I could get someone to look after the new baby for one week I could still manage to go home. The social worker was very understanding and said, 'Talk to me when your baby is born; I'll make arrangements with some foster parents, and one week should not be a problem.'

My sister in law Hannah had offered to look after Katie and Steven while I was in hospital. Hannah had been very helpful and would never question as to why my husband wasn't looking after his kids. I think she knew what he was like and did not want to embarrass me by asking questions.

Millie was three weeks overdue. On my last check-up the doctor wanted me in the next day. I told him no, as I had to make arrangements for my other two children. 'Well, Mrs McGovern,' he said, 'if something goes wrong, we won't be able to help you if you are not here; now go home and sort yourself out, I want you back here the day after tomorrow, so we can keep an eye on you, and if your baby don't put in an appearance soon, we will have to induce you.' I knew Katie and Steven would be happy with my brother Chris and his wife Hannah. Harry had no car at the time, and said, 'I will drop you at the hospital, I'll need to use your car while you're away, to check on the kids and visit you in the hospital.' I did not relish the thought of Harry having my car, but I said ok and told him to look after it, saying, 'I will need it when I get home.' Harry was not one to do much in the line of repairs; his own car had been broken down for weeks, and he hadn't made any effort to get it going.

Following Millie's birth, I was in hospital for a week and could not wait to get home with my new baby. The social worker had been to see me. 'You want to have your baby put with foster parents for a week?' she said. 'Is that still what you want?' I told her no, my baby is coming home with me. Harry had visited me the day after I had been admitted to hospital and I had not seen him since. I wondered why he hadn't been in to see me and our new baby. I had no way of contacting him. My brother Chris and sister Margaret had visited me, but neither of them had seen Harry. Chris seemed angry that Harry had not bothered to visit me, and said that fellow could be anywhere; he is a waste of space. I knew Chris was right, but it was hard to hear him say it.

When the doctor told me, 'You and your baby can go home tomorrow, you are both fine, your husband can collect you after 10 am,' I worried about how I would get home. I could not tell Matron that my husband was missing, so I told her that he had been working away from home and wouldn't be back in time to collect me. 'Don't worry,' she said, 'I will arrange for you to be taken home by ambulance. There will be someone at home with you, won't there? It's our policy that someone is there to meet the ambulance.' I told her yes, my sister would be there.

Chris and Hannah had a spare key for the house, so I rang Hannah to ask her if she could be there tomorrow, as I was being sent home by ambulance. Hannah was there waiting for us, with her own children and mine. They were excited to see the new baby. It was embarrassing for me arriving home this way - everyone around would have seen the ambulance, and would wonder why my husband had not collected me.

After chatting to Hannah, and my neighbour Debbie, who lived across the road, they wanted to see the baby. Hannah said, 'Ellen come into the kitchen, there is something I want to tell you. Chris doesn't agree with me, but I think you need to know.' I said, 'Hannah for goodness sake, tell me what's wrong.' 'It's about Harry,' she said. 'I know Chris told you we had not seen him since you went into hospital, but my brother James had seen him. He came to our house the day after you went in; he had parked your car up the road. As James was walking down the street, he saw that the woman Harry was seeing a couple years ago was in the car. James and him had words. Harry said he wanted to see his children, but James told him no, to F---off and don't come back, so he did. Ellen I am so sorry, but someone told Chris they went on holiday to Jersey that day, so that explains why he hasn't been to the hospital, to see you. I hope you are not too upset.'

And I wasn't - I was furious at him, how could he be such a heartless bastard, I thought, and where is my car? How could he put that bitch in my car? I was so mad I could have gladly killed them both. It was at that point that I realised I actually didn't love him. He had betrayed me yet again, as he had many times in the past; there were no tears, no emotion, just anger. He could hurt me physically, but he could never break my heart again.

Millie was three weeks old when Harry finally turned up. He offered me a feeble excuse: 'I got two weeks' work up the country driving a machine; sorry I did not get a chance to tell you, the money was good, I felt I couldn't turn it down. We were out in the country so I couldn't get to a phone.' I was bursting to tell him what I knew, and said, 'The weather up the country must have been better than it's been here, as you seem to have a great suntan. I know all about where you have been and who with.' I told him: 'Now I want you out of our lives and out of this house. I have already packed your bags for you.' Harry was adamant that he hadn't been away on holiday. 'Someone is filling your head with lies,' he said, but I knew different, I knew who the liar was. Harry knew I couldn't physically throw him out, and though he had no real interest in me and our children, he liked the idea of having a wife and family. If only I had the courage to ask my brothers for help, but my pride and embarrassment wouldn't allow me to tell them how bad things had become.

For the next eighteen years I tried to keep the peace in the house, to make our home as happy as I could for the children and myself. The one advantage I had was that Harry did not spend much time in the house, and we always had a fair idea when to expect him home; in the meantime the children could have fun. I wasn't a great mother and was rubbish when it came to discipline. I would allow them to do anything they liked. They would slide down the stairs in a sleeping bag; we had a settee with a rounded back, and they would tip it up and use it as a see-saw. I enjoyed watching them having fun, and times like that were very precious. Everything had to be back in place by the time their father got home. Harry didn't seem to understand what fun was. He would not allow them to play or make noise; when he was in, he would never allow himself to look happy or smile and be light-hearted – instead he would look for something to argue about. I often thought if the children and I made him so unhappy why didn't he just move out and leave us to get on with our lives?

When Millie was six weeks old I went back to work. I'd got a job in the local school as General Assistant, and found a childminder to look after Millie. It also meant that I could take the eldest two to school, and pick them up, and when they were on holiday I would be home to look after them. Having a regular job meant a great deal to me, and it being so close to home; I had wages paid to me during school holidays, and lots of time off.

In 1979 Margaret Thatcher moved in to Downing Sreet as the new Prime Minister. Some people were excited about having a woman in charge of running the country, but the novelty soon wore off, when she changed the Council tax, to Poll tax, where all wage earners would have to pay a certain amount. She also made other changes that helped many people. I for one took full advantage - council tenants would now be allowed to buy their homes at a reduced price, with the understanding that they couldn't resell the house for three years. I couldn't be more pleased with the prospect of owning my own little house.

In 1980 I applied to Barnet Council for a mortgage, and borrowed the money I needed for a deposit. I was so happy and pleased with myself. At last I had achieved something. As I was working for Barnet Council I had arranged for the repayments to be deducted from my weekly wage - that way I would never fall behind. Harry was pleased I had bought the house. I often listened to him talking to his mates. 'Keeping a wife and family and three kids and a mortgage isn't easy - they are costing me a fortune,' he would say. Him taking all the credit didn't bother me, and I would never contradict him.

I did go back to Cork that year to see my family as I had promised Mom. Harry had suggested we take a car, as it would be easier to manage the three children, and I felt sure Harry would help me supervise Katie and Steven on the boat. I had written to Mom and Dad asking if they would be godparents for baby Millie; we could have the christening back home in our local church, where all her uncles and aunties and I were baptised. Mom and Dad had made all the arrangements for the christening and had a great welcome for us. Being in my old family surroundings made me feel young again, although I was nearly twenty eight, and felt and looked much older. Mom had noticed my weight loss, and had said to me, 'Ellen you look tired and worn out; what you need is a good rest. Your father and I will look after the children for a few days, sure they will be no trouble.' The children were never a problem for me – it was their father who was the problem, but Mom and Dad must never know that.

Our holiday in Ireland was coming to an end, and we were all feeling a bit sad. Katie and Steven loved being on the farm and had a great time. Mom had suggested we go for a walk down the lane to the road, 'and we can be chatting on our way,' she said. I wondered what she wanted to talk about, guessing that it would be something to do with my lifestyle. Mom said, 'Ellen are you happy, I mean with Harry, only I noticed he spends a lot of time in the public house. Sure we have not seen very much of him at all since he's been home. I'm only asking because your dad and myself are a bit worried about you, you don't look happy and you are so thin.'

I had to convince Mom that everything was fine. 'Harry doesn't go to the pub much when we are at home,' I told her. 'It's only because he is on holiday, he could not afford to drink that much – he's got a good job, but it isn't that good. Mom, don't you be worrying about me, I'm fine. It's probably all the travelling that made me look so gloomy, you know I don't like that boat journey.'

'You will be leaving us the day after tomorrow,' she said, 'and I'll miss you very much. You *will* write to me as soon as you get back to London, I'll be anxious to know you got back safe.' 'No tears this time,' I told her. Dad would say his goodbyes in the morning and then make himself scarce. He would never be around the house when we were leaving; that was his way of coping. Mom on the other hand would cling on to the last second, kissing and hugging us, which left me very upset, and I would cry most of the way back to Cork City.

Chapter 14

My brother Sean, whom we had not seen for years, was still missing, and his absence was causing us all a lot of heartache, especially Mom as she would say, 'I wonder if we will ever see him again. Maybe he is dead.' He had been living and working in Swindon, the last time we heard from him, and although we had put a missing people's ad in the Irish papers that were printed and distributed around England, there was no response to any of our efforts in finding him. Sean was working on a farm, outside Cork City, before he came to London. Every time we drove past there, Mom would point to it and say, 'That's where my Sean worked before he went to London.' If we drove past that farm every day, Mom would say the same thing. It was upsetting to hear her; she so wanted to hear from her missing son, to know that he was alive and well. We would all try to convince her that Sean was not dead, and he would turn up eventually.

I knew lots of Irish men who had lost contact with their families in Ireland. Some would say, times were hard and I never managed to get enough money together to go home. Others it was simply, sure, I am no good at writing and as the time passed it got harder and I didn't know what to say to them. It was sad listening to their stories and even sadder, thinking of these poor parents.

Our story did have a happy ending though, because Sean did turn up. He had been missing for ten years. It was amazing, especially for Mom who missed him so much. There was a great big thank you to his girlfriend, Betty, who had encouraged him to get in touch, and had written home on his behalf. Next time we went home, Sean came with us. Mom and Dad were so happy to see him, there were a lot of questions, as to where he had been, and why he hadn't kept in touch, and we were happy, and Mom and Dad's family were complete again. Mom didn't seem to take much notice as we drove past that farm, on the way into Cork City any more. She had her son back and the farmhouse had lost its importance.

It was early summer in 1978: Harry was again out of work. He'd had an argument with his boss and left. 'I don't like driving for other people,' he told me. 'I should have my own lorry, I could make a lot of money, and there is plenty of work out there.' Harry was a good driver and he knew a fair bit about lorries. It was what he enjoyed doing when he could be bothered – in fact we could have been well off. 'Ellen,' he said, 'is there any way we could raise the money to buy a lorry? I know someone who is selling one; I could buy it for a couple thousand. It's a nice clean lorry.' I told him to try the bank, but he said, 'You have a better chance now since you have bought the house.' I told him, 'No, if I borrow money I would be responsible for paying it back, and I could not trust you to give me the money.' He argued that of course he would pay it back: 'Sure won't I be earning loads?' But I knew Harry and I was not prepared to take that chance.

For the next week he was giving me a hard time, trying his best to convince me that it would be the right thing to do, and how it would benefit me and the children. Just when I thought he had given up he said, 'Why don't you ask your sister Margaret for the money? I am sure she would lend it to you.' I said, 'No, you ask her yourself.' The next time Margaret came to visit, he did ask, and after giving her the loads-of-money-that-he-expected-to-earn story, Margaret agreed to give him a loan. Within days he was the proud owner of a lorry, and was very excited about starting his own business, and being his own boss. I was pleased to see him happy and thought this might be the start of a better life for all of us - maybe I can give up work, and be a full time mom, I thought.

The first couple of weeks Harry went out every day, and he seemed to be getting plenty of work. I was delighted for him, and grateful to Margaret for giving him this chance. 'He is going to work every day,' I told her. 'Isn't it great?' Within a month the novelty of having his own business had worn off. He started to make excuses as to why he wasn't at work. I've no work for today he would tell me, but the phone would ring, and someone would ask me where Harry was and why the lorry was not on the site, so I knew he had work.

For the next couple of months the lorry was parked in the local pub's car park, more often than it was out. Then one day he said to me, 'I am going to sell the wagon and buy a JCB.' I was annoyed with him and said, 'Harry just get rid of it, you've given me no money, and have made no attempt to pay Margaret back her money. So sell it and give Margaret her money. Maybe you are better off working for someone after all.' Harry was not going to listen to anything I had to say on the subject, so he sold the lorry and bought a machine.

Harry liked to think of himself as a businessman, but wasn't prepared to put the time or effort into anything himself. He would ring me from the pub and say, 'Ellen, will you go to McGovern's in Willesden and get hydraulic oil for the machine. The driver just rang me, but I've had a few pints so I can't go.' I did run his errands a few times, but the more I did the less he wanted to do. I had my own work, and the children to cope with. So I told him, 'No, I am not going to do your work.' Nothing would come in the way of Harry's social life, not his work or his family. The machine was sold and Margaret got her money back, which I was very pleased about.

I was finding it hard to make ends meet, and decided to find myself an evening job. I knew someone who would look after the children and put them to bed and stay with them until I got home. The Italian restaurant in Golders Green was advertising for a waitress and I got the job. Though I did not know much about Italian food, and found it difficult to begin with, I soon got to know the different dishes, and was enjoying my work. Harry wasn't pleased that I was working four nights a week as it meant he had no one to wait on him; he liked me to be in the house when he got home. I told him, 'I don't have a choice, we've got bills to pay, so until you start bringing in some money, I've got to work.' 'You're only there to draw attention to yourself,' he would say, and would then go on to accuse me of being unfaithful to him. He would get crude and vulgar, and I would tell him: 'I'm working day and night and have not got the energy to be bothered with men. I am only working at night because you are too lazy to get off your ass and go to work.'

It was one row after another, him slagging me off. And I was trying to defend myself. I told Harry, 'All I seem to do is work and look after you and the children, I've no social life and never have any fun.' To my surprise he said, 'Why don't you go out with Margaret on Saturday night? I'll stay in and look after the kids.' I was chuffed that he had offered but not too happy as he had never been left to look after them before, and I didn't feel I could trust him to take care of them now; besides he would probably have changed his mind when Saturday night came. My sister Mary was now married and had a daughter Nicola - I thought that I might ask her to babysit. They could stay overnight. Mary was good with the children; they all loved her, and she lived quite near to me, and we would often help each other.

I enjoyed my night out in the Galtymore club; the band was good and played some of my favourite music, the Beatles and Abba and plenty of Irish music which I loved. I loved dancing – the jive, old time waltz and the Siege of Ennis were great fun. There I could forget my worries, watching all these people enjoying themselves. Having a drink made me wish that I could be more like them. I would never have a drink. Margaret enjoyed a few drinks and would say, 'Ellen why don't you have one, you might like it?' But I would worry about the effects it might have on me; I had to be in complete control. Some people might think I was boring, but living with a drinker made me wary of it.

Harry did find himself a new job and seemed more relaxed. He was going out to work every day, and for a time he was quite pleasant to live with. He could be kind and generous when he wanted, but this kind person could change at the drop of a hat; something could upset him – and it didn't take much – then all hell would break loose. It could be something so simple, like one of the children had moved something from its place, or their shoes were in his way on the floor. Things most men wouldn't notice, he would scream and shout abuse at them, determined to make them cry. I would always defend the children, and distance them from him. I'd send them out to play or tell them to go upstairs. I never let him get away with shouting or upsetting the children; they were good kids, and didn't deserve to be treated badly.

I could take his abuse and often got punched for defending them, but I had to have my say. The first time Harry gave me a beating was about a year after we got married. It was a Saturday night; Harry had gone out but refused to take me with him. I was still up when he came home. I could see he was in a bad mood, and he asked, 'Who have you had in here while I've been out?' I did not know what he was talking about and said, 'No one, I've been on my own all night.' 'I just met a man on the stairs,' he said. 'He was here with you, wasn't he?' I said, 'No, you are talking rubbish,' and went to bed. But Harry was adamant and called me a whore.

Eventually he calmed down and got into bed. He started looking for sex, telling me he was sorry. 'I want to make love to you,' he said. I told him, 'If this is what you call love, I don't want to know, so you just leave me alone.' Harry then sat up in bed and said, 'You don't refuse me,' hitting me with his fist into my face. My nose was bleeding and I had a split lip. Then he raped me. That night I left and walked back to where I had lived with Margaret in St Cuthbert's Road. She was shocked when she saw me with my bloody nose and swollen mouth. She cleaned the blood from my face, and as my bed was still there, she told me to stay the night.

Harry did stop hitting me, but only after he had got into trouble with the police. One time after he hit me, I swore at him, 'If you ever hit me again, I will call the police,' so the next time he went to hit me, I did call the police, though I had no marks, and it was more of a push than a hit, I wasn't going to let him get away with his abuse, anymore. When the police came, they didn't seem that interested in my complaint. It was only when Harry started shouting and swearing at them, that they arrested him for abusive language, and threatening behaviour. He got a fine at Hendon Crown Court the next morning. I was pleased with myself for having the courage to report him. He never punched me after that, though he often wanted to; his fists would come close to my face, but he wouldn't risk the chance of taking it any further.

Harry could be a cruel and spiteful man - like the time I asked him for a cigarette; his friend had called up that morning as I was getting the kids ready for school, and I had no cigarettes. Normally I would take one from the packet without him seeing me, but they weren't lying around so they must be in his pocket. As they both left I went out after Harry, and asked him for a cigarette. He was already in the car, he had put the window down a little, and was taking the cigarettes out of his pocket. As I reached in he put the electric window up, trapping my arm in it. I said, 'Put the window down – you are hurting my hand,' but he just sat there, his fingers still on the button, looking straight at the expression on my face. His friend told him to stop messing around and put the window down. There were tears in my eyes and I felt so humiliated, as I walked away from the car. Harry called me and said, 'You forgot your cigarette.' I didn't turn around; I wouldn't give him the satisfaction of seeing the hurt on my face. I did not get a cigarette, but I did get a bruise around my arm.

I couldn't quite figure out what Harry's problem was. It was like he had a split personality; I never knew from day to day which Harry I had to deal with. Like one time I had an abscess in my tooth, one side of my face was swollen. When he saw it he said, 'Ellen, who hit you? Who's done that to your face?' And I thought he does care about me, but then he went on to say, 'I'm the only one that has the right to hit you like that.'

Chapter 15

That summer the children were looking forward to the school holidays, so they could spend two weeks in Ireland, but I wasn't sure we should go. My dad and I had had a falling out the last time I was home, and he had told me to leave; it was the second time my dad had told me to go back to England. I kept in touch with Mom, and she would write to me often; she would say I am looking forward to the summer, when you'll be coming home again, but I did not know if Dad would make us welcome. My younger brothers Francis and Florence would talk to me on the phone and say, 'Ellen, just come home and don't worry about Dad, he'll be fine.' But I was worried and thought maybe I'll get thrown out again. I knew the children would be very disappointed, but thought it best not to go.

My younger brother Florence was working in the City, and would go home on his day off. Francis was the one who stayed at home, to work on the farm. They were both anxious that we should go home. Then Florence rang me saying, 'Ellen, I've got good news for you. I've bought a house in Cork City. It's fully furnished, everything you need is in it, so why don't you come and stay there for a week or two.' I told him the offer was tempting, and I would think about it. 'There is nothing to think about,' he said. 'Katie, Steven and Millie will love it; it's six bedrooms over three floors. Plenty of space for them to play. Anyway Dad has probably forgotten all about the disagreement he had with you last year.' I remember how cross Dad was that evening, last year. It was the horse fair in town, the time of year my mother dreaded the most. Dad had gone to the horse fair, as he had every year, for as long as I can remember, and would be drunk when he got home. It was just those two days, every year.

The August Bank Holiday weekend, Mom had been on edge all day. 'I hope he don't get too drunk,' she would say, 'or get into any fights.' So when evening came she said, 'Ellen your father will be ready to come home soon, would you go to town and get him.' I found him in his usual pub. Dad seemed pleased to see me, and was ready to go home. I spoke to a few men whom I knew and Madge who was a regular visitor to our house. As Dad and I said cheerio, Madge said, 'John Kelly you can't go yet, stay and have a couple more drinks with me.' It was obvious she had latched on to Dad. She told me to go home. 'Your father is a big boy now, he can look after himself. Where is your mother?' she asked. I told her Mom is at home. 'That's the best place for her,' she said. I could see Madge was drunk, but she was being a bitch. Dad had told her, 'I've had enough drink for today. Mary will be waiting for me.' As we got into the car she came after us. 'John Kelly if you're not staying I might as well get a lift home with you,' she said. Dad got into the back, so I told Madge to sit in the front. 'I'll sit in here beside your father,' she said. I didn't mind giving her a lift home; it wasn't far out of my way – she only lived a mile or so out of the town.

As I left the town I thought the sooner I off-load this woman the better; it was obvious she was flirting with my dad, and I did not like it. Dad had asked her, 'How come you have never met anyone you wanted to share your life with?' 'That's because I never met anyone like you John; now if you were available things might be different,' she said.

When we got to Madge's place I pulled over and said, 'Madge, this is your house,' but she wasn't in any hurry to get out of the car, still talking to Dad, telling him how lonely it was with just her sister to talk to. 'I might go up to your house for a cup of tea, it's early yet,' she said. Dad said, 'Of course, Madge, Mary will be pleased to see you. And one of the lads will drive you home later.' I thought, oh no my mom won't be pleased to see her in that state.

When we got home Mom was preparing dinner for Dad, and said, 'Madge, you will have a bite to eat with us, won't you?' 'Yes, Mary,' she said, 'we had plenty to drink today, but no food.'

Dad was telling us who he had met in town, and who was selling horses, and who had bought. Madge was still talking about her love life or lack of it. 'If Mary ever wants to get rid of you John, you can come and stay with me,' she said jokingly. Mom was being left out of any conversation, and I could see she wasn't happy. As we cleared the dishes from the table, Mom followed me into the back kitchen, and asked me what was going on with 'Madge and your father'. Mom was a bit deaf but knew Madge was paying Dad a lot of attention.

I told Mom, 'Nothing is going on. Madge is drunk, take no notice of her; she was flirting with Dad on the way home, but he was too drunk to even notice. I'll take her home soon.' I went outside to check on the children. I don't know who said what to whom, but Madge stormed out. I called to her, 'I will drive you home,' but she ignored me, and kept walking. Dad had then blamed me for upsetting Mom, and insulting their friend. Dad was really angry at me, and said, 'I think you and your family should go back to London, before you cause any more trouble.'

Maybe it was because of my own insecurity that I had reacted the way I did, and now I was reluctant to go home. I had decided to accept my brother's offer of his house in the city, and after spending a few days there we went home. Florence had spoken to Dad and told him we were home on holiday, and staying in his house in Cork. Dad had asked him, 'Why she is staying up there? Bring them down home.' Dad was happy to see us and did not mention what had happened on our last visit.

I did speak to Mom, and asked her if Madge still calls to see them. 'Oh yes,' she told me, 'that woman drinks too much, and I don't think she knows what she is doing sometimes. She called a few months ago. Your father and I were sitting at the table having our tea; she was sat over there by the fire. I could see she wasn't wearing any underwear, I was so embarrassed, what with your father and your brothers around the place.' I said, 'Go on Mom, tell me what happened.' 'Well it was like your father said at the time, she sat there with one leg in Cork and the other one in Kerry, her modesty in full view.' I was amused and asked Mom if she had said anything to her. 'Ellen, I had to say something, so I said: Madge, you will catch your death of cold, girl, going out this time of year without any underwear. Next time I go to town, I'll pick you up a couple of pairs.' Mom was diplomatic in the way she put her views across, and would not want to embarrass or hurt anybody's feelings. I on the other hand would open my mouth before I engaged my brain and this method often got me into trouble.

Dad had lost interest in farming and hadn't grown any crops for a few years. He had got rid of all the animals, except of course his beloved horses. There were no vegetables or potatoes being planted any more, no corn, barley or hay. The farmyard was looking neglected and bare. It was sad to see how much things had changed, since I was a young girl. Mom and Dad were getting on in years and did not feel able to continue with this heavy work.

My brother Francis was living at home, and doing what he

could but Dad was reluctant to give him a free hand, and allow him to run the farm his way. It was in 1976 that Dad signed over the farm to Francis, much to my mother's delight. And within a few years everything was changing for the better, the old farmyard was being rebuilt. The fields were full of cattle; the farmyard was again busy with the sound of machinery. We were all happy that Francis got the farm. Five of us were now living in London, and had our own careers; none of us were interested in farming. My younger brother Florence was living and working in the City and farming did not appeal to him either. He was a businessman and liked investing in property, though his first job was managing a pub and restaurant on the outskirts of Cork City.

Chapter 16

In 1981 my brother Sean who lived in Swindon, Wiltshire announced his engagement to Betty. She was a Dublin lass. Sean had brought her to visit us in London a few times, and we all liked her and thought what a beautiful looking girl she is. She also had a great singing voice, and would gladly entertain us. Sean and Betty had set the date for their wedding – it was in September 1981 and we were all invited. Katie, Steven and Millie wanted to go to the wedding with their dad. I was six months pregnant with our younger daughter Maria and had decided not to go.

I wasn't happy to let the children go with their dad. He will be drinking I thought and wouldn't look after the children, and besides I would have to buy new clothes for them, which I couldn't afford. Millie was only four years old and would not go anywhere without me; Katie was happy to stay at home, but Steven was really anxious to go to the wedding. My sister Margaret said let him go, sure I'll look after him, but even Margaret could not prevent what was to happen on the evening of the wedding.

Harry, Steven and Margaret set off for Swindon mid-day; the wedding was at 3pm, so they would get there in plenty of time. I had said to Margaret, make sure you keep an eye on Steven; I knew Harry had no patience with children, and I could not help worrying about my boy.

As the wedding reception was in full swing that evening, Harry had started chatting to the bride's niece and before long it looked like they were an item: she was sitting on his knee, Harry had his arms wrapped around her. Margaret had seen what was going on, but Steven had not taken any notice – he was playing with other children who were at the wedding. My brother Sean and his bride Betty were busy making sure everyone was having a good time, and had not noticed what Harry was getting up to. My sister Margaret was keeping an eye on what was going on, so when she saw Steven, sitting with his dad and this girl he had befriended, she felt things were getting out of control. She could see Steve was crying and felt she needed to rescue him. His dad had told him, 'You must be nice to this woman, she might be your new Mummy.' Steven had told his dad, 'I don't want a new Mummy, and I won't be nice to her.' Steven was only ten at the time and very much a mummy's boy; his father had no time for him, and rarely paid him any attention, so when his dad suggested getting him a new mom, and then being nasty to him, was just too much for the little lad to take. Margaret had taken Steven outside to talk to him, and calm him down, but he wanted to go home.

Margaret rang me from Swindon. It was about nine in the evening, and straight away I knew something was wrong. She was asking me if I could get someone to pick them up. A taxi would cost more than we could afford. There was only one person I could ask to make that journey and that was my sister Mary's husband Joe, so I rang him, praying that he would be home and hoping he would say yes. I'll give you some money for petrol I told him, and, thanks to Joe, Steven got home safe. It was a lesson for me not to let the children go anywhere with their dad again, unless I was with them.

Harry arrived home two days later, as if nothing had happened, saying, 'I don't know what all the fuss is about, I was only messing with Steven. He took me up wrong; I wasn't with that woman, we were just talking.' I told him, 'That's a pity, I was hoping you would stay in Swindon with her, and not come back here anymore.

You're no help or use to us.' And here I am expecting another baby for him - I must be as mad as he is.

I remembered when I told him I was pregnant, he said, 'How did that happen?' I said, 'Oh in the usual way,' to which he replied, 'Don't be smart; I mean whose is it?' I asked, 'Whose do you think it is?' 'I don't know,' he said, 'Bill Kavanagh is around here a lot, or maybe Baldly Tom.' We had both known Bill and Tom Moran for many years - they were friends of ours. Bill was a mechanic, and bought and sold old cars. Whenever my car broke down I could ring Bill, and he would come and fix it, and if he couldn't get me mobile he would always have a spare car to lend me. Harry would watch me push my car down the road in the morning to start it, and would say I must put that battery on charge for you, but it would never get done. He would mean to do it but something more important would come up and my problem would be put on the back burner. Unlike Harry I could always depend on my friend Bill Kavanagh, but that's all he ever was - a friend.

Harry knew the baby I was carrying was his. Telling himself it was somebody else's made him feel better about his own actions; he would often accuse me of being unfaithful, and convince himself it was true. That way he could justify his own betrayals, and in that he was an expert. For the next couple of weeks Harry and I did not talk much to each other. My baby girl, whom I had already named Maria, was due the middle of November, and soon I would be on maternity leave from my school job. I worried about who would look after the children while I was in hospital. Millie would be my biggest problem; she was seven and was always very close to me. Katie and Steven could stay at home, and my friend Debbie MacAndrew, who lived across the road, had offered to get them up for school and keep an eye on them in the evening.

I was hoping that if everything went according to plan, I would be home in two days. Katie was then thirteen and very sensible, Steven was twelve and could be a bit boisterous at times, like all boys at that age. My sister Margaret was in a job at the time, but she could take Millie to work with her, and had offered to look after her for a few days. She would bring her to the hospital every day to see me; I was happy with that arrangement and knew that Millie would get the best possible care.

On my last visit to the ante-natal clinic, my doctor was concerned about the way my baby was positioned. He told me she had flipped right over and was now in an upright position. 'We will turn her around,' he said, 'and let's hope she stays there,' but she didn't and as I left the hospital that day, I could feel her turning again. The doctor had told me she was in no danger, but, 'it's not possible for you to give birth with her in that position. I will see you in two weeks. Then we will decide what course of action to take – it may be a C section but don't worry about it for now.' For the next couple of weeks I hoped this baby of mine would get herself into the right position; I would often talk to her, telling her the trouble she would be in, if she didn't sort herself out. I knew if I had to have a C section I would be in hospital for at least a week. And that was too long to leave my other three children.

On my next hospital visit nothing had changed, as far as the baby was concerned, and I had been given a date to be admitted. It was 22 November 1981. I only had a few days to get everything sorted out at home, to make sure there was plenty of food for Katie and Steven, mainly things they didn't have to cook. I had given my neighbour Debbie school money that she would give them every day, and a bit extra just in case they wanted to buy something. I told Katie and Steven, 'Now you have to be good while I am away, keep out of your father's way, and don't cause any arguments.'

As I was giving them the do's and don'ts, there was an knock on the door; Katie got up to see who it was. 'Mom, it's for you,' she said. 'There are some people that want to talk to you.' When I got to the front door, there were three people outside. I don't know who those people are I thought, and wondered what they wanted. 'Can I help you?' I said to the woman who was standing nearest to me. 'Sorry to disturb you,' she said, 'we just wanted to know what day next week you're moving out as we've got to make some arrangements. I am sure you will understand what it is like.' My first thought was, these people have the wrong address, and I said to her, 'I think you have the wrong house.' 'No, it's the right house,' she said, 'Harry, your ex-husband told us we could come and have a look around. He said you and the children were moving out, and our daughter was moving in here with him, we wondered if you were leaving any furniture or carpets.'

For a few seconds it was like I had been struck dumb. I could not believe what I was hearing. My first reaction was had the children been listening at the living room door, as kids do. After I checked I turned to her and said, 'I am sorry you have been misinformed, we are not going anywhere, and neither you nor your daughter will be moving in here, this is my house now go away' (with a few choice words here and there) – that was a habit I had whenever I was really angry, the swear words came out, and now the woman was also angry, and told me, 'Well if that's the case, you keep your husband away from our daughter.'

After they had left I stood there for a minute in disbelief. I couldn't let the children see how shocked I was. Hopefully they did not hear the conversation I thought, as I went back into the living room, trying to look as normal as possible, but Katie knew something was wrong. 'What did those people want to talk to you about Mom? I know there is something wrong.' 'It's not important,' I told her, 'I'll tell you later.'

That night I didn't get much sleep with everything going around in my head. How could this be happening to me? It is one thing after another, I thought. I'm going into hospital in two days' time. Would Harry bring this girl into our home, when I wasn't there, and already I knew the answer, it was very likely that he would. I need to tell Katie I thought, she was thirteen years old, and should be told what was going on. I had to give her instructions on what to do if the worst happened. Her Auntie Mary lived near us. I told her, 'If things don't work out, take your brother Steven and go and stay with your auntie.' This was a terrible situation Harry had put me in, as if I did not have enough to worry about. I told my sister Mary, and asked her to look after Katie and Steven, if they were not happy at home. Mary was happy to help and assured me that everything would be fine; 'I'll make sure of that,' she said.

As I left home for the hospital the next day, depressed and anxious, I could only hope that everything at home would work out. I had driven myself to the hospital; it was about four miles away, and the nearer I got the more stressed I became. My doctor came to see me that afternoon. 'How are you, Mrs McGovern?' he said. 'I want to check you over, and do a scan. We need to see what position the baby is in now, has she moved again do you think?' I told him she had. 'Let's have a look,' he said, scanning my stomach and showing me her on the scan. She had gone back to her original position, and now she had her hand behind her head. 'We will get your labour started, and hopefully we can turn her later. If that

does not work, I'm afraid it's going to be a caesarean tomorrow.'
I did not mind that, but it meant a longer hospital stay which is
what I did not want.

That evening when visiting time came and loads of people
descended on the ward, as I wasn't expecting any visitors I decided
to nip home; the nurses wouldn't notice I thought, with all the
people around. Putting on my dressing gown and slippers, I
headed for the exit I had parked near, and hoped nobody would
notice me getting in the car. As I drove home I started to think
about the medication I'd been given early that day, and wondered
how long it would take to work. Would I get back to the hospital,
before I went into labour, and prodding my unborn baby
daughter a couple of times, I warned her, don't you dare move,
until I get back, and smiled to myself as I pictured her sitting
there with one hand behind her head. Almost like an adult sitting
on an armchair relaxing. Katie and Steven were in the house,
and everything seemed to be fine. They had not seen their Dad
since getting home from school. Katie said, 'Mom you shouldn't
be here, we are fine, don't be worrying about us, now get yourself
back to the hospital.'

All the visitors had left when I got back. The sister in charge
said, 'Mrs McGovern, where have you been? We have been looking
for you. You were due your medication.' I told her, 'Sorry, I was
bored and went walk about.'

The next morning the doctor and midwife tried in vain to turn
baby Maria and release her arm. She had no intention of budging
from her comfortable position; they decided I would have a
caesarean section. I woke that evening and found I was having a
blood transfusion, and thought God I am going to be in here for
ages. Maria was beautiful with a mop of dark hair; my other three

children were all blond. I was in a high dependency room, with a wonderful black nurse looking after me. Because I wasn't able to look after Maria myself, she was kept in the nursery. Having a caesarean back then was a painful experience, the cut was from hip to hip; nowadays it's no more than a few inches.

My sister Mary brought the children to see me and the new baby that evening. Mary said, 'Katie told me you sneaked out of the hospital last night and went home to check on them; well I am going to sleep in your house every night until you get home. I did not realise you were that worried.' I was so grateful to Mary, now I could relax and not worry about Harry and the woman he was seeing. He would not bring her to the house if my sister was staying there. My other sister Margaret was bringing Millie in to see me every afternoon; she seemed happy and I knew she was being well looked after. My brother Chris and his wife Hannah had offered to help any way they could. I have a wonderful family I thought, I should be happy, but my biggest problem was still at home - my husband.

My nurse was so kind and caring, above and beyond what she was paid to do, she was my true guardian angel. She would ask, 'Ellen, are you in pain? Is there anything I can do for you? You don't look too happy.' I thought I have been here before, and thinking back fifteen years ago, when my baby son had died, and my own life was in danger, I didn't want to think about that now, but I still missed my little boy, and wondered what he would look like now, a fifteen year old. Back then married life was new to me, and though Harry had treated me badly I believed he would change, and settle down. But what is the saying, a leopard never changes its spots, and that was my husband Harry. Nothing had changed: I was still being abused and raped by him as he saw fit.

And now here I was with another beautiful baby daughter, and nothing to offer her, except a very unhappy home. I was feeling sorry for myself. My wonderful nurse told me, 'Ellen, I think you might be suffering from post-natal depression,' but I knew it wasn't that; it was despair and desperation.

I did not want to go back to 94 Clitterhouse Road, the house I swore nobody would ever make me leave, after being evicted from my last home and left standing on a street corner, with two babies and nowhere to go, waiting for social services to come and rescue us. Now I was telling my nurse I didn't want to go home. 'I know,' she said, 'you're not well enough, you'll have to stay with us another few days at least, that wound is still very raw, and your stitches won't be taken out just yet.' 'No,' I said, 'I don't want to go home ever.' She sat on the edge of the bed. 'What do you mean?' she asked. 'Sure you will have to go home; you got three other children waiting for you and of course your husband.' 'That's the problem,' I told her, 'we don't get on.' 'I see,' she said. 'Now you get some rest. I will get someone to have a proper chat with you later.'

I did get to talk to a social worker, a very nice man who informed me that he could arrange for me and my four children to go to a safe house for women who had been beaten by their husbands. Though I hadn't been exactly beaten, he would still recommend that they take us. The nearest one available was in South London, which was miles away. If I accepted it, it would mean my eldest three children, would have to change their schools. I wouldn't be able to travel back to my job. The offer was not what I had hoped for. I had no choice now, I would have to go back home, and anyway it was my home, the home I had put together from bare floorboards. I was not thinking straight, why would I let Harry and his girlfriend take it from me?

I was discharged from the hospital on 30th November 1981 and though I was looking forward to being with my family, I was sad leaving the security of the hospital, and the nurses that were so kind to me and looked after me so well, but it was time to go home. It would be Christmas in three weeks and I had a lot to do. Harry was kind to me in the days that followed, and helped look after the baby. The incident with his girlfriend's parents was never discussed; I did not see any point, I tried not to think about it.

Katie, Steven and Millie were doing everything for the baby. In fact I was not getting a look in, which suited me, as I was still very sore and needed to rest. Harry was still not working, and my wages were paying the mortgage and the household bills, which left us with little for food. It would be Christmas in a couple of weeks, and the children would be expecting some presents. I asked Harry to get a job; 'We need some money for Christmas,' I told him. 'There is no chance of me getting any work until after the New Year,' he informed me. 'Well in that case,' I said, 'you can borrow money from someone to tide us over until I go back to work.' 'Who do I know that would lend me money?' he said. 'Anyway I would not ask.'

So it was up to me as usual to do the providing for all of us. I wasn't due to go back to my job until the end of February. I would have to find temporary work somewhere. My sister-in-law Hannah knew someone who had just left a job, working at night in a factory. The hours were from 9pm to 1.30am. 'Why don't you go and ask if they are looking for someone?' she said. I got the job, but it was so near the Christmas holidays, they wouldn't need me until after the New Year.

It was great that I got the job, but it wouldn't be any financial help to me now. I would have to go begging to the social security office in Willesden, and that was something I didn't want to do. But, I thought, if I don't, the children won't have anything for Christmas, not even a decent meal. It should be Harry that was applying to them for help, as head of the family, but he had refused. Now I would have to lie to them, and say my husband was no longer with me. 'Maybe I will ask them for a loan, and I could pay it back later.' Having no money to put petrol in the car, I would have to walk to Cricklewood, which was about a mile, and get a bus from there. It had been snowing the past couple of days, and I worried that I might slip and fall. My stomach was still sore after the caesarean. I would have to be very careful. On arrival I was shown into a cubicle, where I explained my situation, and after being questioned for nearly an hour, and made to feel like a beggar, the gentleman in question agreed to give me a one-off payment. 'You will get a cheque in the post in a day or two,' he assured me.

We all had a good Christmas and I was able to buy something for the children but that feeling of betrayal and rejection was still there, creating an atmosphere which I couldn't seem to shake off. It was like Harry had invaded my home with this girl he had been seeing, and I couldn't get it out of my mind. I started work in the factory in January 1982. My daughter Katie would look after baby Maria and give her the ten o'clock feed. I would be home in time for her next feed at 2am. Maria was a very quiet baby who rarely cried, so long as she was fed, and changed. Katie would keep her in her bedroom until I got home. Then I would put her on my bed, still in her little sleeping bag.

Having been back to the hospital for a check-up, I was physically fine, but I had been having nightmares which left me exhausted. Coming home after my night shift I was tired, and would look forward to getting home and to bed, but almost afraid to go to sleep. I would say, 'Please God, don't let me have any nightmares tonight, I am so tired.' The dreams were always the same: I would be standing outside, with my three older children, and my keys wouldn't open the door. I was shouting through the letter box to Harry to open the door. Then as I stood back to look up at the window, I could see Harry and his girlfriend standing there; she was holding my baby Maria, he had his arm around her shoulder, they were smiling. I was shouting up at them to let me in. He had opened the window, and told me to go away, 'These are my family now,' he was telling me. I would be screaming, crying and begging him to give me my baby back. 'You can keep the house,' I was telling him, 'just give me my baby.' Katie, Steven and Millie were crying, saying, 'Mummy make Dad give us back our baby.' At that point I would wake up, and glance over my shoulder to check that Maria was there and safe. It was only a dream I would tell myself, wiping away my tears. It was like they wanted to take everything that was dear to me.

In another dream, I would be standing inside the window, Harry and this girl had set my car alight, they were dancing around it, and laughing. I could not understand why this girl in particular was bothering me so much. I did not even know her name. She wasn't the first; none of the others had got inside my head to this extent. I knew in my waking time that my dreams were ridiculous, but I had no control over what was happening in my sleep. Knowing that I couldn't continue like this, I wasn't eating properly, and now I was afraid to go to sleep, I decided to go to see my doctor; maybe she would give me something to stop these nightmares.

I couldn't tell my doctor what the nightmares were about - it would sound silly and embarrassing for me. 'I think you have post-natal depression,' she told me. 'I will give you something that will help.' I told her I wasn't depressed. 'I am fine during the day, it's just when I go to sleep.' 'What I am going to give you will help you get a good night's sleep. Be careful,' she said, 'these drugs can be addictive. Come back and see me in two weeks.' She just did not understand. This wasn't a sore throat, the flu, or an infection, I was telling her about, I had wasted her time and mine. There was no cure for something that was in my head; maybe I should have gone to see a psychiatrist.

I would be going back to my day job soon. I had found someone to look after Maria. I had been spending too much time in the house, and felt sure that going back to my school job would be good for me. It would take my mind off the situation at home and I needed the extra money. Maria was settled with her baby minder, Katie, Steven and Millie were at school, and I felt well enough to go back to work full time. I still had my night job. I wanted to clear all my debts before I would give that up.

Chapter 17

It was in March 1982 after another explosive row with Harry, the children and I moved out of the house. I just could not take any more abuse, and see my children getting so upset because of Harry's cruel attitude. I had spoken to my sister Margaret and asked her if she had a room to let; she owned a house in Willesden, in which she let out rooms. 'If one becomes available could we have it?' I asked. 'I have a room empty but it isn't very big,' she told me. 'It's got two single beds. You're welcome to it,' she said, 'but how are you and the children going to manage, in such a small room?' 'It will be fine,' I told her. 'Katie and Millie can have one bed. Maria in her cot, and Steven and I will take turns to sleep on the floor.' The next day I packed a few things, picked the children up from school, and moved to Willesden. It wasn't ideal, but it gave us some peace, and I needed some time to think. Margaret would not take any money for the room which was a blessing, as I would still be paying the bills for Clitterhouse Road.

It was during the time in Willesden that wearing seat belts in the car become compulsory. It was also around that time that the police had found human body parts in a house in Cricklewood. Melrose Avenue was the road where many young men had lost their lives at the hands of Nelson. It was a sad time for everyone, and as I had to drive past the end of Melrose Avenue each day on my way back to Cricklewood, thinking about the young men and their families put things into perspective and I realised my life was not that bad after all. The nightmares I'd been having for months were getting less and less frequent, and now I wasn't afraid to go to sleep.

We continued to live in Willesden for the next couple of months; it wasn't the best and I did feel a bit sorry for my two eldest children. They felt restricted, and were missing their friends, with no garden to play in, and little space in the room. There was a lot of bickering going on between them, which was understandable. I knew that I would have to go back to Clitterhouse Road eventually, but I needed this break away from Harry, and I was enjoying the freedom it gave me. Maria was getting too big to sleep in her carry cot; she needed a big cot, but there was not enough space in the room.

Harry had visited a couple of times, mainly to give me some bills that had come to the house. He wanted us to come home with all his usual promises, which I had heard a hundred times before; his promises meant nothing to me now. The children wanted to go home and I would have to put them first. Besides my sister Margaret was out of pocket with us living there rent free. Within hours of us moving back home the house was full of children. The four boys that lived across the road were in. The bikes were being taken out, and the football was bouncing around the road. Watching them playing and laughing made me realise how selfish it was of me to take them away from their home and friends. I knew their father would never show them any love or respect. So I would have to try harder, to protect them and keep the peace. But for me I knew there would be a price to pay, and that was something I did not want to think about.

It would not take much to make Harry angry, but if he was in a good mood, the kids could wreck the house and he would not say a word to them - if only I could keep him in a good mood all the time, how happy we all could be. I wouldn't have to worry about the ball that was bouncing around the road one minute, and coming through the window the next, as it did on many occasions. But Harry could never know or be told about such incidents. I would set off to the glass shop on Cricklewood Broadway, with my measurements, and hope that I could have the new glass fitted before he got home. Being grateful that it was not a neighbour's window, and lucky that the panes of glass were small and would not take long to replace them. To make sure that he wouldn't notice the wet putty, I would get a wet tea bag, and rub it all around.

I remember one evening the children and I were watching television, when Harry came in. He had been shopping and bought himself a pair of shoes. As Harry opened the box to show us, Steven said, 'They are a nice pair of shoes, Dad, how much were they?' Harry immediately started on him, saying, 'It's none of your business how much they were. It's my money that paid for them.' He went on about how ill-mannered Steven was, and badly behaved, he kept on imitating Steven's words over and over again. I would always take Steven's side, and after all Harry was making a big deal out of nothing, which was him all over. I think sometimes his conscience would bother him, because he would never buy anything for his family, except the odd bag of sweets.

Little incidents like that would end up with me and him having another blazing row. Him calling me a good for nothing whore, along with any other choice words he could muster up. 'One more word out of you,' he would say, 'and I'll put your fucking head through that window.' I knew that would not happen now; he had punched me many times in the past, grabbing me by the hair so I couldn't get away, but that had not happened for many years – he couldn't take a chance of getting himself arrested again. Back in the 60s and 70s domestic violence was rarely in the media and the police weren't interested, so nobody cared if your husband was beating the shit out of you; he was your husband so that made it ok. But now in the mid-80s all that had changed and Harry knew that. He had other forms of abuse more intrusive. A beating would have been more acceptable to me. I would often say to Harry, 'One day when the children are grown up and left home, I will leave you, and make a better life for myself, and you will end up a lonely old man.'

I sometimes try to think back on happy times we shared, and it is difficult - good times are very scarce in my memory. In fact from the moment that wedding ring went on my finger the good times were all in the past. I was now owned for his use only. It was no different to when my dad would buy a horse at the fair, only that Dad was kind to his horses. If he had been working the horses, ploughing or whatever, he would stop mid-day, and say, 'These horses are getting tired; they need to be rested for a while' - which is more than Harry ever said to me. I would have loved to hear him say, 'Ellen, you need a break, you're working too hard,' or 'sit down I'll do that for you'. It would be more like, 'Why has that not been done, you lazy bitch?' So if I were a horse I would have been treated better.

The family had outgrown our two bedroom house. Steven was twelve and needed his own bedroom. My brother Chris had divided the biggest bedroom into two, but that still did not give us enough space. I spoke to my brother Sean who still lived and worked in Swindon, about the possibility of building an extension, and what it entailed. Sean told me, 'Ellen, if you can get planning permission, I will get it built for you as cheap as possible.' I got the drawings and applied to Barnet Council. My first attempt was turned down. We needed a double extension, to give us a larger kitchen and two more bedrooms. I was disappointed but felt I must not give up. I'll go and see someone in the planning department in person, maybe I could persuade them, I thought, and they might understand why we needed more space.

The man I spoke to was sympathetic and assured me he would do his best to get it passed, and he did – within a couple of weeks I had a letter in the post granting me full building permission, to go ahead within the next five years. I was really excited; all I needed now was the money to build it. I re-mortgaged the house which gave me enough money for the materials and other expenses. My brother Sean found a builder in Swindon who was willing to do the work for a weekly wage, and Sean would buy the materials that we would need in Swindon. It would cost less there, he had told me. Harry bought the blocks, which was his contribution; he was pleased the building would soon get on its way.

It was two years after permission was granted that the builders started work. And for the next couple of months, everything was a mess. We had to sleep in the living room, kitchen, in fact anywhere there was space for a mattress. My son Steven got the worst place; it was on the kitchen floor and with no back wall to the house, and he had definitely got the short straw. I had promised him his own room, one of the new ones, I told him, so he was happy with that. There was a lot of building up, and tearing down that summer. But none of us minded that much; we were looking forward to the end results, which made it all worthwhile.

Jim Hasett was the builder's name. We all got on very well with him, and I could see he knew what he was doing; he was good at his job. Jim was travelling from Swindon to London daily. He needed to stay in London Monday to Friday, but we had no space for him. I phoned my good friend Bill Kavanagh – he might be able to find us a mobile home, I thought. I needed enough space for two builders I told him; within a few days there was a two berth mobile home parked in our driveway. It wasn't just the builders that used it – the children and their friends would spend hours during the day playing in it. They loved it and would often have tea and sandwiches out there. With Maria and myself regularly joining them, to be honest I was enjoying the change of scenery as much as the children.

Harry and the builders did not get on too well, and he would criticise the work Jim was doing – not that Harry knew much about building work: he had never even hung a picture on the wall for as long as we lived there. Now he was going around with a spirit level telling me that the floor isn't level or that wall isn't straight. 'You had better have a word with that builder,' he would say. I would tell him, 'You have been in the pub most of the day, there is nothing wrong with the floors or the walls, it's you that can't see straight. Stay away from the pub tomorrow, and then you can see more clearly.'

Harry had to criticise, he just could not help himself. Jim would ask me, 'How do you put up with that husband of yours? He is a bully. I'm doing this job for you and your brother Sean, who is a good friend of mine – that is the only reason I am still here. I would not normally take that crap from anybody, but, Ellen, if he pushes me too far, I may have to flatten him.' I told him 'feel free', but I knew as I said it, I wouldn't want Harry to get hurt, though God knows he often deserved a beating. Jim did finish the work. I was happy with our new home. I had a big bright kitchen, a shower room, and the children had their own bedrooms.

Harry got himself a job and things were going well for me, he was giving me money on a regular basis, and seemed content at work, and at home. There were no rows and we all felt more relaxed; with all the extra space, the children were out of his way, which is what he would want. He liked to be in control of the television, and would only want to watch programmes on ITV. Sometimes if he was asleep on the settee, Katie or Steven would switch over to another channel; if it wasn't on ITV when he woke up, he would scream, 'Who switched over that television, put it back where it was.' Even when he was asleep he still felt the need to be in control.

The extension to the house had been completed some time ago, but there was still work to be done. We had no central heating, just a gas fire in the living room. I could now afford to get that done. My friend Bill had still not taken away the mobile home he had lent us, and Harry was complaining that it was still on our drive. 'I will put it out on the road,' he told me. 'I need to put my car in the drive.' I told him, 'The children still play in it, they won't be happy; it's been here for the past two years.' 'It's time Bill came and took it away,' he said. I could not see any harm in it being there, after all there was plenty of parking space for all of us.

A few weeks later I wished Bill *had* taken it away. It was a Saturday afternoon, the children were all out playing around the road, as Harry was walking down the road on his way back from the pub. He went to the van and though there were other boys and girls in there, he picked on Millie. 'Get out of there, you little whore,' he shouted, marching behind her as she crossed the road. She was screaming, crying, I could hear her from inside the house, calling to me. I ran out to see what had happened to her. Harry was there shouting, 'Get in the house you little whore, and don't let me catch you in that van again.' I said, 'What's wrong?' Harry told me, 'She's been messing around in the mobile home with the boys.' I screamed at him, 'Leave her alone. She's thirteen years old and they're doing no harm. There are lots of kids in there.' 'Well,' he said, 'this little whore won't be going in there again.' I told him, 'Don't you call her that,' but he wasn't about to stop, and as Millie ran up to her room, he followed. I was blind with fury. Running to the kitchen, I grabbed a knife from the drawer, and followed up the stairs. Harry was still shouting at her. 'Come out here, I'm not finished with you yet,' he said. When he saw me with the knife, he said, 'This has nothing to do with you.' I said, 'It's everything to do with me. I'm not having you abusing my daughter. Now you apologise to her or this knife will end up in your gut.'

He looked shocked and realising I had gone past anger, he had taken a few steps back. I screamed at him, 'I will use this knife, now tell her you are sorry.' Opening Millie's door I said, 'Your father has something to say to say to you.' 'Maybe I went too far,' he said, 'but it's for your own good.' 'That's not an apology,' I told him, taking a step towards him, still with a firm grip on the knife. I said, 'Now try again.' This time he did say 'I am sorry for what I called you, I did not mean to upset or embarrass you in front of your friends. I am really sorry'. Even a forced apology was better than none, and it made Millie feel better. I could listen to his foul mouth name calling and so on, but when it came to my children I see red. I had not thought about the consequences if I had used the knife on him and at that moment I would have used it. Thinking about it later, I was glad I didn't have to. If anyone wronged or abused my family in any way, I found it hard to control my temper.

There was one occasion when I went to see a teacher in my son's secondary school; the teacher had caned Steven, breaking the skin across the palm of his hand. Steven had not shown it to me for a couple of days, by which time it had turned septic. I was livid; no one had the right to inflict such punishment on a child. The teacher in question had a reputation of being harsh, and wasn't very well liked. So, after school one day, a group of boys decided to throw flour at him, and the next day he chose Steven to take the punishment. I was so angry though Steven did not want me to go to the school. 'Just leave it, Mom,' he said.

But the more I thought about it the angrier I got. This is actually grievous bodily harm I told myself; he is not going to get away with it. I am going to the school. My plan was to go straight to his classroom, but it was a big school, and I did not know which classroom he was in. I would have to ask someone for directions. The deputy head was in his office. 'Come in,' he said, 'can I help?' I told him which teacher I wanted to speak to. 'Is it about your son Steven?' he asked. 'Mrs McGovern, your son Steven is doing OK but he needs to spend more time on his homework.' 'Mr Parker,' I said, 'it's not about Steven's education.' I told him what had happened, and said, 'I need to speak to his teacher.' 'I can't allow you to do that,' he said, 'but I promise you I'll deal with it, this should never have happened.'

I was angry and disappointed that I could not see this teacher face to face, after rehearsing on my way up what I would say to him. I wasn't happy and as I left Mr Parker's office I said, 'Please give him a message from me - if he ever touches my son again, I'll wait for him outside the school, and I'll break his two effing legs.' I often asked myself why I couldn't be brave all the time - when it involved someone within the family I wouldn't give an inch; yet when it came to Harry, I was a coward; was I that much afraid of him, or was I afraid for my children? I allowed him to get away with so much, not saying a word, often trying to humour him, to get out of a situation, when really I should be throwing everything in the kitchen at him, but my nature and my quiet personality would not allow me to be aggressive. Besides, one angry person in the house was enough for the children to cope with.

Katie, Steven and Millie were now in their teens, and would have their friends coming to the house. The last thing they would want to hear was their father and I bickering at each other. Harry wouldn't exactly welcome their friends with open arms; it would be the opposite in fact and sometimes he would be downright rude to them, so much so that Katie avoided bringing her friends to the house. It was the same if somebody rang to speak to them; he hated the children using the phone, especially Katie. It would not matter that sometimes it would be an incoming call which did not cost anything. Sometimes he would unplug the phone and put it in the boot of his car. What he didn't know was that I had a spare phone, hidden in the garden shed. As Harry went out the front door, the spare phone would be coming in the back door. He did not confiscate the phone to save money, or that he was worried we would get a huge bill in and not be able to pay it. Harry never paid the phone bill or any other bill for that matter. It was a statement: I'm in control and you will do as I say.

I left my job in the school in 1984. A friend of ours who worked in construction sites had rung me. 'There is a big job starting in Bethnal Green,' he said. 'We are looking for someone to do the catering for the workmen. Ellen, you could make big money here. If you want it, the job is yours.' I arranged to go and visit the site; it was on Bethnal Green Road, a huge factory that was being converted into luxury flats. After being shown around by the site agent, who was encouraging me to take the job, he said, 'You will be here for at least two years, and if you need help that can be arranged.' I thought what a nice man, how could I not accept, it was like I'd hit the jackpot. 'You can earn more money here in one day, than you could in a week in your school job,' he told me.

It was a wonderful offer I thought, but did I have the courage to take on such a big job? I would be catering for at least a hundred men. I needed a few days to think about it, I told the site agent. After a discussion with my family, who seemed to think it would be a great opportunity for me, I gratefully accepted the job. I knew it would be a little different from what I had been doing in the school, but after a few days I knew that accepting this job was one of my better decisions. Everyone on the site seemed very relaxed, with little or no health and safety issues. I could take the children to work with me, if one of them was off school because of illness – it would usually be Millie; she hated school and would try every trick in the book, to get a day off. From the time she opened her eyes in the morning, she would cry, begging to stay off school. 'You don't understand, Mom,' she'd plead. 'I'm not well, I have a headache.' So she and her quilt would end up on the back seat of the car, as I set off to work. Her condition improved as I neared the site. I loved my work and the people I worked with. I continued with this kind of work for many years, and made a good living from it.

When Steven was fourteen his father got him a job in the local club, picking up glasses. 'It will be good for him,' he told me. 'It will make a man of him and he will earn a few bob for himself.' This kind of work was not what I had wanted for Steven. I told Harry a drinking environment was not a good place for a fourteen year old. I was very much against the idea, telling Harry,

'He is too young,' but Harry argued, 'I had to work when I was his age.' Steven was excited about earning his own money and also pleasing his dad. He craved his dad's attention and approval all his childhood, and now he would be spending time in his dad's circle of friends and for a young lad that was exciting. Harry was soon boasting to me, 'I gave Steve a beer and he loved it,' or if Steve bought his dad a pint out of his wages, 'that's my boy,' he would say, 'it's about time he bought his dad a drink.' That was not what I wanted to hear, I worried for Steven and hoped he wouldn't be a drinker - could he not see what drink had done to his father? Steven especially had so often been a victim to his father's abusive language.

I was worried for my son: his homework wasn't getting done and he had lost interest in school. I had tried so hard to get his father to see sense. 'Steven should not be working there on school days; Friday and Saturday is enough for him,' I told Harry. 'Let him be,' Harry said. 'He is enjoying being in the club with his dad, and if he has the odd drink it won't do him any harm.' But it did do him harm. His attendance at school got less and less. He finally left school at fifteen and found himself a full time job, mixing with men much older than he was, and doing things they would do, like going to the pub after work. I did not have any influence on him anymore. So for the next couple of years, to my disappointment, Steven would often come home drunk, and was often in trouble with the police - mainly for driving offences, and always drink related. He was disqualified before he was old enough to hold a driving licence, but I consoled myself with the thought that Steven was still a teenager, and would soon see the errors of his ways. Boys need a man's influence to guide them in the right way. That is something Steven missed out on. He did eventually move on and his drinking habits changed, and he grew up to be a kind, good-hearted, caring young man that any mother would be proud of.

Having made one last attempt to keep the family together, and save my marriage, I told Harry that if he didn't treat us better and stop fighting with everyone in the house, I would divorce him. 'Do what you like,' was his response, so we were divorced in 1986. Harry did not even bother to turn up for the hearing, and full custody of the children was given to me. Harry had dismissed the whole thing and told me, 'Catholics can't get divorced, so you're wasting your time, you are not going to get rid of me that easy.'

My solicitor had written to Harry advising him that he should move out of the marital home. 'I'm not going anywhere,' he told me, and after a meeting with the solicitor I learned that I would have to go to court and apply for an eviction order. The solicitor asked, 'Can you afford to pay for a hearing? I don't think you will get legal aid on this occasion.' 'I can't pay,' I told him. 'Don't worry, we'll fill in this application form and see what happens; you may be lucky,' he said, but I was not lucky, and legal aid was refused, so that was it - nothing seemed to be working out for me. I had my hopes set on what the solicitor had told me. 'It will only take a couple of months to get your husband evicted,' he had told me, and now I had lost all hope of getting him out of my home.

I was so disappointed and so was my eldest daughter Katie, who was always asking, 'Why you do put up with him, mom? Throw him out.' This was the little girl who stood at the front gate crying for her Daddy to come home. She was about two or three then, and now a teenager, she couldn't stand the sight of him. 'Ask your brothers to throw him out,' Katie would say. 'I'm sure if they knew what was going on they would gladly come over from Ireland to help.' That I didn't doubt – they already knew what he was like, they had seen how brutal he could be, on many occasions when we were home on holidays. Harry couldn't even behave himself in somebody else's house. I knew Katie was right; I did need help, but I did not feel comfortable about involving my brothers in my domestic affairs. It would be another six long years before Harry finally moved out of the house. In the meantime the children and I coped with the unpleasant situation as best as we could.

Chapter 18

Life can be so cruel sometimes, and it's the good people that suffer the most, as it was with my dad one Sunday in April 1988. Mom, Dad and my two brothers had just got home after being at mass, when my dad had a stroke. He was taken to the regional hospital in Cork. I hoped and prayed that he would recover; I flew to Cork to see him and to be with my mother, knowing how upset and worried she would be. He was her soul-mate; she would be totally lost without him, as we all would.

Dad did recover, but he was left paralysed down one side, not being able to walk or do anything for himself. It was heartbreaking for all the family, especially for Mom as she could not do much to help him. Dad was a big man while Mom was petite and would be unable to lift him; besides, Dad's personality had changed: he was always an easy going type of person, and now he was angry with everyone, including his own family. Though I didn't think too much about why he was behaving so out of character at the time, I can now relate to his plight. He was a man who was used to farming the great outdoors, his beloved horses, decision making, his freedom, and now he found himself in a wheelchair, and he had lost everything. It was no wonder he was angry, he had every right to be. He was only seventy two and a very active man. How could God let this happen to our dad? What had he done to deserve such punishment? It broke his heart when he was told he couldn't live in his own home anymore.

My younger brother, his wife and children lived in Cork City. Dad didn't like the residential home he had been in, so Florence and his wife Mary decided to make the adjustments to their home to accommodate a wheelchair, and other things that Dad would need, so he could come and live with them. Dad wanted to go home back to the farmhouse which was impossible, so this was the next best thing. It wasn't home but he was with his family, where he would get the best possible care. Mom and Dad lived there for a couple of years. The five of us living in England had a rota set up between us, so that we would each spend two weeks every summer in Ireland, and take Mom and Dad back to the farmhouse. It worked well - as one of us was due to leave, another one would arrive. My brother Francis and his family lived near the farmhouse. They would help with Dad, lifting him and so on, during the summer. The old farmhouse was getting shabby and damp with no one living there most of the year; that's when my sister Margaret suggested bringing Mom and Dad to London. 'I've got plenty of room,' she said, 'they can come and live with me.' They had been to London a few times on holiday in the past. Mom loved it but Dad wasn't impressed. The big City wouldn't be of his choosing back then, but now everything had changed, and we were confident that he would settle down.

Margaret's house was in Neasden, and we all lived within a couple of miles' radius, so we could all help, but Margaret would have the hardest job. She worked as a carer, looking after disabled, terminally ill and elderly people. 'I'm well used to this kind of work,' she would tell me, 'it's like having another patient to look after.' My younger sister Mary lived in Cricklewood and looked after Mom and Dad for a short time, but with three young children, she was finding it difficult and they returned to live with Margaret, where they stayed for the next two years.

I was now renting a cafe in Cricklewood; it was a small place that I rented from the railway. It had been closed for a few years, and needed a lot of work doing to it, but I was determined to make it a success, and after getting a loan from the bank, I set about getting it refurbished and ready to open. I was excited about the prospect of having my own business. Harry didn't approve and kept telling me, 'You're wasting your money, Ellen, you won't get any customers there, and it's in a bad place.'

Harry wasn't working himself and as he did not approve, he was not going to give me much help restoring the café. I wanted to prove him wrong and on my first day of business, there were lots of people coming through the door, passing trade, local business, and others coming in to have a look. Gradually the business was improving and with lots of regular customers, my hard work was paying off. I was making a good living, and spent the next eleven years in that little café, on Claremont Road; though I loved working there it wasn't all happy times.

Harry would be in every day sitting in the corner, giving orders. 'This man is waiting for his tea,' or 'why has that person not been served yet,' he would say. My staff and I were more than capable of serving everyone in turn, but Harry would have to put his oar in letting everyone know who was boss. He never seemed to do any work of his own these days, and I hated to see him in the café. That was my project and I did not want him there. Living with him was hard work, but having him watch me all day was unbearable. I opened at five am, and closed at four pm. It was a long day and I didn't need Harry's negative input. He would talk to lorry drivers, who would say, 'I never thought I would see you in this kind of business. Have you given up driving?' 'Yes,' Harry would say, 'the wife wanted this place, so I thought I would give it a go.' I would think to myself don't you give the wife any credit, will you?

One morning Harry heard me getting up for work, and said, 'I'll come to the café and give you a hand.' I told him, 'I don't need any help this time in the morning, I can manage fine on my own,' but he insisted. When we got to the café, he went straight for the kettle to make himself a cup of tea. As I started switching everything on and filling the urn with water from the tap, Harry went into the store room to fetch some tea bags. 'Come in here,' he called to me. 'What's wrong?' I said, thinking he couldn't see the tea bags. 'There on the top shelf,' I told him, as I walked into the store. 'Look at that,' he said, pointing to a single tea bag that was on the floor. 'Why is that on the floor?' he shouted. 'Are you trying to draw mice around the place?' 'It's only a tea bag,' I said. 'Why are you are making a big deal of it?' But he carried on. 'You're one lazy fucking bitch,' he shouted. I couldn't take this abuse at five in the morning; the tears were rolling down my face. I was tired - I had only got up half an hour ago and already he was upsetting me.

I glanced at the clock on the wall - it was five twenty. Mick Tierney will be here soon, I thought, I can't let him see me crying. I'll get some onions out and pretend that's what made me cry. Mick worked in the dairy further along the road. He was a neighbour of ours and had often been in our house. He would pop his head around the door every morning at 5.30 to say hello, sometimes staying for a cup of tea.

That morning when Mick arrived, he was surprised to see Harry, saying to him, 'I'm glad to see you here. It's not very safe for Ellen being here on her own these dark mornings.' Looking at me, he said, 'What's wrong, you look like you have been crying.' I told him, 'No, I have been chopping onions.' 'I'll stay and have a cup of tea,' he said, as he took a seat at Harry's table. 'Is one of you going to tell me what's wrong?' Mick asked. 'Why is Ellen upset and don't tell me it's the onions.' Harry told him: 'It's nothing. I had to give her a ticking off earlier,' telling Mick the reason why. 'If the Health Inspector came in and saw that, they could close us down,' Harry told him. Mick said, 'Let me get this right, Harry. You upset Ellen over a single tea bag? What the hell is wrong with you?' As Mick was leaving, he turned to Harry and said, 'You need to get yourself a job, and leave your missus to do what she does best.'

Harry sat in that café day after day, weeks, months and I hated it. I could not talk to the customers in a friendly way but only in a business-like manner. I knew the customers would think, she's not very friendly, and that wasn't me, but I knew Harry would be watching, so having a joke and a laugh would be more than I dared do.

Harry did eventually find himself a job, but in the meantime I would have to supply him with money. Every day at closing time he would have the hand out. 'Give me a few bob so I can go for a drink,' he would say, and to be honest I was glad to get rid of him for a few hours, so the children and I could have a bit of peace. It would be on the very rare occasion that he would get home before eleven. That would give me time to cook dinner for the family, help the children with their homework, and any other jobs that needed doing. Harry's dinner would be put to one side, until he got home, and if he was in a good mood he would eat it; other times he would say, 'What's this shit you're giving me? Do you expect me to eat that?' Often times he would throw the lot on the floor.

Trying to keep Harry happy was hard work; if he was in that kind of mood, he would criticise everything – the food, the state of the house, in fact I could not do anything right. What the rest of us had for dinner would not be good enough for him. I would shop according to what money I had, fish fingers, sausages would often be on the menu, for the children and me, but that would not be acceptable to Harry. He would say, 'Ellen, is it too much trouble for you to go and get a few chops for a man's dinner?' It wouldn't dawn on him that maybe I hadn't got the money to pay for them. Did he think the butcher was going to supply us with meat for nothing? If Harry spent as much money on food, as he did in the pub, we would all be eating well, but that would never happen.

On the odd occasion Harry would come home sober, whatever we were eating would be fine for him also. Harry could be kind and agreeable, and I would often look at him and think to myself why can't you see? I would feel sad for him; there is a good man in there somewhere, I would tell myself. Why can't he be happy with what he has got, what else is there, why can't he see what is happening to his family, why can't he realise that he is much more likeable when he is sober? I had discovered many years ago that Harry couldn't socialise, unless he had a few drinks first. Any social event that we as a family had ever attended Harry would have to be drunk before we set out on our journey, which made me nervous; I knew that another couple of drinks would change his whole personality. People would avoid talking to him, all our friends and family knew what he was like, and it would be only a matter of time before he would get aggressive towards someone; for that reason people tried to avoid him. Yet when he was sober, he would be the life and soul of the party and everybody was his friend, and would want to spend time with him.

I remember some years ago our children were still very young; in fact Maria was only a few months old. My brother Francis was getting married back home; the wedding was in Limerick, and as he had sent me the money for our fares, there was no reason not to go. All my brothers and sisters would be there, as would Mom and Dad, my auntie and cousins, and of course neighbours that I grew up with. I had been looking forward to the wedding and seeing all my family. I had hoped Harry would not want to go, the children and I would have a much better time without him, and to begin with he had told me that he wouldn't be going, which pleased me, but at the last minute he changed his mind. 'I'm coming to Ireland with you,' he told me. My heart sank knowing full well that he was sure to cause trouble, and spoil the wedding for all of us. I did not want to go if he was coming with us, but I couldn't let my brother down on his big day. I told Harry, 'Don't you get drunk and humiliate me in front of my family.' He assured me he wouldn't. 'I won't be drinking,' he said, 'I promise you.' But could he keep his promise? I hoped so; it would mean we would have a great weekend or a weekend from hell. Unfortunately it was the latter.

We had all been staying at the same B&B, the entire family. Harry had gone out the morning of the wedding. 'I am just popping out for a packet of cigarettes,' he told me, but as time went by and he had not come back, I knew he had gone for that all important pre-event drink that he always felt he had to have; he could not wait to start drinking at the reception with everyone else. Harry seemed to be in good form for most of the day, but by evening, I could see his mood changing. He had started picking on Steven, watching his every move; though Steven wasn't doing anything wrong his father had chosen him; it could have been anyone, and he did not need to have a reason.

By the time we got back to the B&B that night, Harry had

insulted most of my family; they had all been trying to calm him down, to humour him, without success. My younger brother Florence had tried to distance Katie and Steven from their father; they were both crying, but Harry turned his anger on him, saying, 'They are my children, mind your own business,' swearing at him. Florence was adamant and said, 'If you fancy your chances, try and stop me,' walking off with Katie and Steven. Then it was my turn. 'You're going to be sorry for this when I get you back to London,' he told me. I said, 'Harry, what can you do to me that you haven't done a thousand times before?' He had once again ruined what should have been a wonderful day.

We returned to London the next day, humiliated and embarrassed at the way my husband had behaved. I had hoped that with all those people around he would show some dignity and self-respect; he had shamed himself and all our family. That's one of many incidents I can't forgive him for plus some of the things he's done in the past – whenever there was an occasion or family get-together after that episode, if Harry wanted to attend, then the children and I would stay at home. I often wondered if Harry was in fact an alcoholic or just a heavy drinker, or at what stage you define the two. I had on many occasions in the past suggested that he should get professional help, but he would angrily dismiss the idea, saying 'Can a man not have a few pints, without you calling him an alcoholic?'

Steven and Katie were both working at this stage and would be either out or in bed. Steven would say to me, 'Mom, I am going to find my own place, he is driving me mad, I can't be listening to him anymore.' I didn't want Steven to leave home; I felt he was still too young to be living on his own. For a time I managed to talk him out of that idea, but I knew sooner or later he would go, and I understood why – after all, I would have done the same given the opportunity. I still had Maria and Millie at school; they still needed me so there would be no escape for me yet. I would tell myself one day somewhere in the future it will happen, and I'll be free. It was getting harder to hide the pretence of a happy home; Mom and Dad had been living in London for some time, and would ask questions about Harry, where he worked, what he did in his spare time, were we happy, questions that I didn't have answers for. I knew they were suspicious, that indeed everything wasn't as rosy as it should be. But I couldn't tell them the truth, and I made sure the children or anybody else wouldn't tell them; they would be so hurt and disappointed. They could not fix it, so it was best they did not know.

My sister Margaret worked two evenings a week in her job. I would go and care for Mom and Dad on those evenings; getting Dad out of bed for his supper, he would need a wash and be given his medication. At this stage Dad had become very helpless, and as he was a big man, getting him in and out of bed was hard work; I would worry in case I let him fall. When Dad was tucked up in bed for the night, Mom would say now the three of us will say the rosary together. Mom was still as holy as ever; I don't think, there was ever a day in her life that she did not say the rosary.

I left Neasden at nine thirty one evening; I knew Mom and Dad would be fine – Margaret was due home any minute, it had been a long day and I was anxious to get home. I had been home only a short time when the phone rang; it was Harry. 'I need a lift home,' he said. 'Could you come and pick me up from the club?' It was only fifteen minutes' walk, but Harry would not walk anywhere. I asked, 'Are you ready now?' 'Give me ten minutes, to finish this pint,' he said. I had a few things to do, the washing up needed doing, and the dogs hadn't been fed - I'd do that and go and get him, but just as I was ready to leave, he came in. I could see he was in one of his tempers. 'You're one lazy good for nothing bastard,' he shouted at me. I told him I was just about to leave, I had been looking after Dad this evening. 'I had only got in when you rang.'

Harry wasn't going to listen to excuses, as he continued with the verbal abuse; Steven and his friend came in during Harry's outburst. 'What's wrong?' Steven said. 'Why you having a go at Mom?' 'She's a lazy old whore,' Harry told him. I could see Steven was getting angry; the more he told his dad to stop, the more he went on, until Steven could not take it anymore. 'It's nothing to do with you what goes on, between your mother and me,' Harry told him, 'so fuck off and mind your own business.' With that Steven went to hit his dad, he grabbed hold of him with his fist clenched. 'You're not going to get away with abusing my mom anymore,' Steven shouted, as his friend grabbed hold of him and pulled him off his father.

This was the first time any of Harry's family had dared to stand up to him, and he was shocked. After that night Harry made damn sure Steven wasn't around when he felt like dishing out abuse. Steve and his friend left the house that night. 'Come and stay at my house,' his friend had said, but without my knowledge, my son had one more job to do before he went anywhere - as he hadn't taken his anger out on his father, he would take it out on his father's car. He went around the car kicking it as he went; every panel was dented either from his feet or his fists. I wouldn't want Steven beating up his father, that would go against nature - as for the car, I felt Harry was a deserving victim. I must admit I was proud of my son on both accounts.

Next morning Harry came in to the café. 'Did you see what your son done to my car?' he raged. 'Don't you mean our son?' I replied. 'Well I'm going to report him,' he told me. 'He's going to pay for this.'

Harry went to the plumber's yard where Steven was working that morning, telling the gentleman he met what Steven had done, and recommending that his son should be sacked from the job. Steven would be going to the yard, at 8am, to pick up his van; he would usually pop into the café on his way past, and this morning especially I was anxious to see him. I had not spoken to him since he and his friend had left the house the previous night, and as he was upset then, I wanted to make sure he was ok. I did not have long to wait, Steven arrived in the café with a big grin on his face, telling me what his dad had done that morning. 'Don't worry, Mom,' he said. 'Dad thought he was talking to the boss, but it was actually the night watchman.'

I was disappointed that Harry would do that to his own son, but not surprised. At that stage Harry realised he wasn't dealing with children any more. They had been bullied by him for so long, but they were now in their teens, and were ready to fight back; I didn't need to protect them anymore.

I also felt stronger knowing that I had a backup if I needed it. Harry could never change even if he wanted to - that's how he was, having been the boss, the controller, the bully for so long, and now his own family were growing up, he realised he couldn't control them anymore, and that wasn't going down well with him. He would blame me. 'It's your fault,' he would say, 'it's the way you brought them up, and you spoiled them, now they have no respect for their parents.' 'Harry,' I would tell him, 'you never showed your children any respect, how can you expect them to respect you? You reap what you sow; you have always been hostile towards them, so don't be surprised now when they retaliate.'

Chapter 19

It was nearing Christmas in 1990 that Harry came home from the pub one night. I was in the kitchen. He said, 'Sit down, Ellen. I want to tell you something.' He seemed happy and I wondered what this was about, what he was going to tell me. Then he said, 'I've met a very nice woman, and I really love her, but there is a problem, she's married. Her name is Kathleen. I've been seeing her for a few weeks now. Her husband has been treating her badly, so she left him and her two children.' My first thoughts were that's rich coming from a man who treated his own family so badly. My second thoughts were, would they be setting up home together, and as I asked him hoping the answer would be yes, he shook his head telling me she hasn't told her husband about me yet, it's early days. I was happy for him, thinking if he's with her then he won't be pestering me. I had not been sleeping with him for quite some time at that stage, though he was still trying to get me back into his bed – he could not accept that the relationship was well and truly over.

His news was a great relief to me. I was not going to allow him to abuse me in that way anymore; it was over a year ago that I had made a promise to myself. He was behaving in his usual way, coming home drunk – whether I was asleep or not wouldn't make any difference to Harry – and he would start his usual performance. I would have to spend the next couple of hours fighting him off. I would get up in the morning feeling I had not been to bed. As I set out on my way to open the café at 5am one morning I told myself, you can't go on like this, you don't deserve this kind of treatment, it will have to stop. I had only slept for two and a half hours, and I felt shattered. That day as I closed the café, I told Harry that I needed to talk to him, telling him how I felt. I said, 'Harry, please let me sleep tonight, I'm so tired. If you wake me when you get back from the pub, I swear it will be the last time. I will get out of that bed and I won't be going back.' Harry told me he was sorry. 'You won't hear me getting into bed tonight,' he said. I knew Harry - he would think about this conversation later as he sat in the pub, and he wouldn't take too kindly to any threats I had made. That night I did leave his bed, and kept the promise I had made to myself, never to go back.

Now that he was in a new relationship I was happy for him, and also for me. Kathleen was also a heavy drinker, like Harry. They had that in common at least, and I wished them well, and hoped everything would work out for them both. About six months into the relationship, there were still no signs of them living together, and the new woman in his life was getting too cheeky for my liking. She would phone our house on a regular basis, to talk to Harry. To begin with I was polite to her on the phone, and would tell her not to ring the house phone, to ring him on his mobile, but when she persisted I would hang up if it was her.

Our youngest daughter Maria, who was nine at the time, would often answer the phone, and shout, 'Dad, it's your girlfriend.' I felt it wasn't right and caused many arguments. My behaviour towards Harry had changed, and these days I wouldn't let him get away with anything that resembled bullying; in fact now I was the bully, and was finding it difficult to be polite to him. I had on many occasions in the past told Harry, 'I'm not asking you for anything, all I want from you is that you are kind to us, and stop treating us like you have been in the past, like we are the enemy.' When I married Harry all those years ago, I took my vows seriously; I thought we would be together for the rest of our lives, grow old together, for better, for worse, but there is only so much of the worse a person can take, and I had had my fair share.

So one night being woken up by all the commotion in the bathroom, I quickly went to investigate. As I stood at the bathroom door, there was Harry climbing out of the window, one leg in the bath and the other on the outside of the bathroom window. For a few seconds I just stood there thinking should I let him carry on, knowing that he would land on the concrete yard below, and would most certainly be seriously hurt - or lead him back inside to safety.

It was rare that Harry would sleepwalk, and this was the first time he had put himself in danger. I could not let him fall, so I took him by the arm and led him back inside, asking myself did I hate him that much that I would allow him to fall - obviously not. I resented his presence; I would sometimes look at him and think why me, why did you pick me, with all the girls around Cricklewood and the Galtymore at that time, why was I the unfortunate one, the one you chose to use and abuse, why couldn't it have been somebody else, thinking I wouldn't wish my past life on anyone, I still thought why me? Did he see me as someone he could intimidate, control - which is what he had done? I was moulded to be the person he needed, the provider, housekeeper, the mother of his children, the person who kept his bed warm, but never the lover, the soulmate. A term I was referred to was the wife, not my wife, and I now realise that Harry never loved me. Did he even like me I wonder?

My brother Sean, who would sometimes come to visit, still lived in Swindon, so he would stay with us overnight. It was during one of those visits that Kathleen rang the house phone, wanting to talk to Harry. It was Sunday morning and we were in the kitchen having breakfast. Maria had answered the phone, and came running out. 'Dad, it's your girlfriend again, she wants to talk to you.' Sean looked at me and smiled, it was obvious he thought it was some kind of a joke. Harry was on the phone for ages, his breakfast still on the table. Sean asked, 'Ellen, who is he talking to?' I told him, 'It's his girlfriend Kathleen.' 'Are you joking?' Sean said, looking at me again. 'You can't be serious.' As I nodded, he asked how long it had being going on. I said this one in particular many months, but in general as long as I can remember.

Sean stood up, leaving his food; he was angry. 'Ellen,' he shouted, 'why didn't you tell me what was happening? It's not just you he is making a mug out of, he is taking the piss out of the whole family.' I asked Sean to calm down. 'There is nothing between us for years,' I told him. 'That's not the point, Ellen,' Sean said. 'He is still living here, why are you such a pushover? Why haven't you kicked him out?' 'I have tried on many occasions,' I told Sean, 'but he refused to go. What can I do?' 'Well he will go now,' Sean said, 'with a few kicks up the hole if necessary.' Sean was very angry and asked, 'Does Chris know what's been going on here, does any of the family know?' I told him, 'Not really, it's my problem.' 'Not anymore,' he said. I told him, 'Sean, please don't cause a row. Maria is in the living room and Katie, Steven and Millie are still in bed, after a late night.' I didn't want them to hear what was going on. 'Don't worry, Ellen,' Sean said. 'There will be no shouting in here, I promise.'

As Harry returned to the kitchen, he immediately realised that Sean knew everything. 'Who the hell do you think you are?' Sean said. 'How dare you, have you got no morals, no self-respect? This is the end, Harry, now get out of this house, and take your belongings with you.' Harry turned and walked out to his car. Sean followed telling him that 'it's over, find yourself somewhere else to live. I will be back in two weeks; don't let me find you here'. Harry returned home late that evening. He wasn't pleased that I had told my brother. 'That's my business,' he snapped. 'You have spent half an hour talking to your girlfriend on the phone,' I told him. 'Sean asked and I told him. I'm not going to lie or cover up for you anymore. You must find yourself somewhere else to live.'

Harry did not move out for several months after, but he did eventually decide to go and live with Kathleen. It was summer 1991; a great weight had been lifted, I was so happy but there was also a tinge of sadness. Maria was only ten and I wasn't sure how she would feel. She was the only one of the family who had any kind of relationship with her father; I had hoped that bond would continue. Harry would be still living in the area; she could call and see him. I wouldn't want Maria to be unhappy; our eldest three were all in their teens, they had their jobs, a social life, their friends coming and going. They would all welcome this final split like I did.

That final day back in 1991 was overwhelming. When Harry was gone, I sat down for a few minutes to gather my thoughts, this was what I had wanted for so long, and now I felt lost and confused. Where do I go from here I thought, then I said to myself come on Ellen, no more headaches, no more panic when you hear the key in the door at closing time, for whoever comes through that door from now on will have a smile on their face, you can chat and laugh with your customers in the café, go to the Galtymore, do everything that you daren't do in the past, have your life back. After telling myself all the these things, there was still a great sense of loss.

After moping around for a couple of days, I told my sister-in-law Hannah, that Harry had gone. I hadn't told Chris or my sister yet. Hannah asked, 'Ellen, why are you looking so gloomy, you should be happy, isn't that what you wanted?' I told her it was. 'I feel a bit lost and I don't know why. Hannah, you probably think I'm mad,' I told her, 'and I know I should be jumping up and down with delight.' 'Give yourself a week or so,' Hannah told me. 'Harry's been in your life since you were a teenager, you are bound to feel a little unsettled, think of all the unhappiness he caused you. Come and pick me up on Saturday morning,' Hannah said, 'and we will go to Portobello Road market – that should cheer you up.'

I loved going down the Portobello Road with Hannah, she loved looking at the old furniture, in fact anything that was old, she had a great eye for old jewellery, and we would always end up buying a few things. Then it was into a wonderful cake shop for tea, and some of their delicious cakes, which Hannah would always insist on paying for. I loved walking around the market, which was a real treat for me. By the time I left Hannah that afternoon I was feeling much better. As she got out of the car at her house, she turned to me smiling and said, 'Ellen, will I send Chris up to your house, to change the lock on your front door?' As I drove away I laughed to myself, only Hannah would think of such details, and of course I knew she was right – the locks would have to be changed. For me and my family this was a new beginning.

Within a few weeks of the final split I was feeling more confident, in control, I didn't feel owned any more, I wanted to put my arms in the air and shout I'm free. I would skip around the house in the evening and think how happy and content I felt, why had I spent the best years of my fife in such an unhappy marriage. I should have found a way out; I should have swallowed my pride years ago, and told my family, asked them for help. None of them knew the true extent of the situation - any one of them would have helped, or indeed all of them. I didn't have to suffer in silence, I had chosen to. Thinking back now, religion had played its part - what God has joined together, let no man pull apart - so I guess that is why I couldn't involve my family, it wouldn't be fair to ask them to choose between me and God.

Now I had to look to the future, I had the café and was financially comfortable; I also had a wonderful family - all four of them had turned out better than I could have ever expected. Considering the parents they had, a dad that was always drunk and a very unhappy mother. If I were a child and could choose a dad and mom, it wouldn't be Harry and me. Sometimes I look at them now all grown up, and think how lucky I am, and I feel so very proud.

I think back to when my own mother was in hospital, one evening as she was talking to the doctor, telling him where she came from, and how many children she had. 'You know, doctor,' she told him, 'my family have some of the best jobs in London.' The doctor smiled at her, and said, 'You must be very proud of them, Mrs Kelly.' 'Oh I am, doctor,' she said, and now that is how I feel about my family.

Chapter 20

Dad and Mom went back to Ireland in the summer of 1994. Dad had been getting more helpless, and wanted to go home; he needed 24 hour care, and was eventually accepted in a care home in Cork City, where he passed away two years later, on 29th February 1996. He was a good man and a loving father, and I miss him greatly.

Two years before my dad died, my sister-in-law Hannah was diagnosed with terminal cancer. It was a great shock to us all; I was devastated. Hannah was a good friend, and had helped me in so many ways over the years. My brother Chris would be totally lost without Hannah; their three sons were grown up and doing their own thing. I was worried about Chris – he was very much a family man, who would spend his evenings indoors, not much for socialising and rarely went out for a drink. He and Hannah would often come to visit me, and other members of the family.

Within a few weeks of losing my dad I could see how poorly Hannah had become. The hospital doctor had told the family that there was nothing more they could do for her, other than make her comfortable. I was about to lose a second member of my family, within a very short time. It seemed so unfair – Hannah was only 52 years old; during the few weeks Hannah had left I spent as much time as I could in the hospice with her, still hoping for a miracle, that she might be saved. And though it wasn't what I wanted to hear, Hannah would talk freely about what she wanted to happen after she had gone, where she wanted to be buried, who she would want to come and see her remains in the funeral home. 'My own family only,' she would tell me. 'I don't want it opened to everyone. You'll keep an eye on Chris and my boys, won't you?' she would say.

She was a strong-willed lady, who accepted her fate, and could talk about anything, while I would sit there and listen with tears rolling down my face. 'You stop that crying,' she would say, 'and sure we'll all meet up again one day.' I asked Hannah if it was possible for her to let me know that she was OK. 'Give me a sign,' I told her, 'and I will know that it's you.' I also asked her to say Hello to Dad and give my baby son a big kiss from me. After the funeral I waited for the sign, that would let me know that she was happy, but it never came. Two years later my niece who hadn't been well, woke up in the night to find Hannah standing at the foot of her bed. 'I wasn't frightened,' my niece told me, 'I was wide awake. I only saw her for a few seconds.' So I guess that was my message, Hannah was fine, she sends the message through somebody else. Maybe she thought I was too weak, that I'd be frightened. I do believe that good people go to heaven and my sister-in-law was a good person.

My mother had come back to live in Neasden with Margaret and I would see her often. I would collect her every Saturday and we would go shopping together. We would also visit Hannah's grave and a decade of the rosary would be said before we left, then it was back to Chris's house, to do some cleaning, washing and whatever was needed doing. My brother Chris wasn't very domesticated, and Mom loved to help. 'Men are no good at that sort of thing,' she would say, and everything would be spick and span before we left. Last would be to make sure Chris had a perfectly ironed white shirt hanging in his wardrobe for mass on Sunday.

I had been living a single life for the past few years at this stage, but Mom still didn't know. I was enjoying the freedom and peace of mind, our house was a peaceful place now, and I was happy. I couldn't bring myself to tell my mother the truth about Harry and me, knowing how hurt she would be; she would have her own opinion on the situation and would not understand. I could almost hear what she would say, 'Ellen, you must stick with your husband through thick and thin, no matter what.'

Katie, Steven and Millie were grown up now and were encouraging me to go out socially. 'Why don't you go to the Galtymore?' they would say. 'You are always talking about it, there is no reason why you can't go out and enjoy yourself.' 'I don't like going out on my own,' I would tell them. 'Ask Auntie Margaret to go with you,' Katie would say. I did eventually start going out, but it felt a bit strange. I was uncomfortable being amongst all those people and nervous of my surroundings; there was no reason why I felt so out of place and old. I had not been to a dance hall for many years and had forgotten how to relax and enjoy myself.

The Galtymore looked different; it wasn't how I remembered it; a new hall had been built and the whole place had been updated. The main hall had a beautiful balcony which stretched right the way around, and that is where I would spend many nights looking down on people enjoying themselves, and afraid to venture down myself. I would always tell the girls what a great time I had. They would be asking, who did you meet Mom, anyone you knew, did you get lots of dances, did anyone ask you for a date? Unbeknown to them I did not have the courage to dance with a man nor go alone on a date - that would definitely be out of the question.

Then one Saturday night after getting my glass of coke, I headed for my usual spot on the balcony; there would always be lots of people there, going to the snack bar and drinks bar. As I stood there watching all the couples, floating around the hall

underneath me, I noticed a man standing beside me. He said,
'Hello, are you enjoying the night?' I answered him politely,
and looked away. He continued to talk, about the band that was
playing, about the size of the crowd that was here tonight, and
then came the usual question, 'Where do you come from?' I
told him I came from Co Cork. He said, 'Sure I am virtually a
neighbour of yours, I come from Co Clare, I've been coming to the
Galtymore for years.'

He told me he lived in Peckham, South London. He said, 'I
like this place, so it's worth the journey, and it's somewhere to go
on a Saturday night. He added, 'I know all the faces here, but it's
recently you've put in an appearance, and always on the balcony.
My name is Michael, most people call me Mick, and what's your
name?' I told him my name was Ellen. I felt comfortable talking
to this man, he was much older than me, well dressed and very
polite. He told me he had never married. 'I never met anybody
that would have me,' he said, 'and now women seem to think I'm
past it; I get a lot of no thank yous, when I ask them to dance. I see
that your glass is nearly empty, please let me get you another one,
I'd feel bad coming back with just a drink for myself, it's only a
drink, no strings attached.'

As he queued at the bar, I thought what a nice person he was,
but then I thought back to the last man whom I thought was a nice
person and look how that ended up, how wrong I had been. When
Michael came back with the drinks I was deep in thought. 'Do
you mind me talking to you,' he said, 'or would you prefer I was
not here?' 'Sorry,' I said, 'you're fine. I was miles away.' 'Anywhere
nice?' he said. 'Not really,' I told him.

Michael talked about when he came to London in the 50s, what
it was like about his work, his family back home. I found him

interesting as he talked about his life and a girl he once met and hoped to marry. 'But things went wrong between us,' he said, 'and she married someone else. I never bothered much after that, once bitten and all that. Ellen, enough about me, would you do me the honour of giving me one dance, please don't say no, we will do a couple of rounds of the hall down there, and I promise to bring you right back here after.'

Reluctant as I was I couldn't refuse this pleasant man one dance, and as we walked around the balcony and down the stairs, I thought what if I've forgotten how to dance, it was an old time waltz, what if I had forgotten the steps, it would be so embarrassing. He said, 'Ellen, I forgot to tell you, I've got two left feet.' I laughed and said, 'Well, thank God for that.' When the dance finished he escorted me back to the balcony, saying, 'thank you very much, it was really nice talking to you.' As he walked away he said, 'Maybe I'll see you again sometime.'

That was the first of many nights that I would see Michael. He would always find me, whether I was upstairs on the balcony or down on the dance floor, always stopping to talk. 'Come on,' he would say, 'let's have a dance, or two.' I often wondered why this nice respectful man never asked me for a date, maybe he realised how shy I was, and he was being kind, or if he had asked me out, would I have gone... I don't know - maybe.

Chapter 21

It was nearly a year since my dad and my sister-in-law passed away. My brother Chris had started to go out socially, and would invite me along. He liked going to a pub in Willesden on a Monday night; it was called Ned Kelly's; there was music and a little dance floor. Chris took great care not to dance with anyone except me; he would worry about what people might say, or think - not that his late wife would have minded Chris going out, she would not have wanted him to stay at home and be lonely. I would say, 'Chris, you know most of the people here, there's no harm in you having a dance. I mean it's not like you are looking for another woman.' 'Of course I'm not,' he would say, 'but those people might think different: he only buried his wife last year, and there he is looking for a replacement already, that's the kind of thing people might say.'

So now both of us felt out of place: me worried in case I bumped into my ex-husband, and Chris worrying that people might think badly of him. Chris would come to the café every day, and we would discuss our problems at great lengths. 'I don't care what people think of me,' he would say, 'and you shouldn't worry about Harry. If he comes anywhere near you, I'll soon tell him where to go.' Such courage when discussing our problems in the café, over a cup of tea - what a pity our brave ideas did not extend to our social life.

I knew eventually Chris would move on - he was a smart looking man and, although he was not interested in women at that time, I knew a few that would have snapped him up given the chance - one in particular who often said to me, 'Your brother is so handsome, and he walks so elegantly, someone like him would not give me a second glance'. 'Chris is not like that,' I would tell her, 'he isn't a snob, and the reason that he walks like that is, because as a teenager he spent some time in an army training camp, it was only for a couple of weeks every year, that's where he was taught how to stand and walk properly.' As youngsters back home, we would laugh at him and make smart comments. At the time we thought he was funny. Chris loved the time he spent in the army barracks in Cork, and had benefited a great deal from his experience there. It's only now that I see why women would find him so attractive - to me he was just Chris.

Maybe sometimes I was a little jealous of his popularity. I would just blend into the background, nobody seemed to notice me, except for one or two men, who knew my ex-husband, and thought they might slip into his place - a free home and someone to look after them. One of them in particular was very persistent, and would follow me around. Nowadays this action would be called stalking.

He would tell me, 'Ellen you need a man around the house, I'll look after you.' I would think to myself, am I so unattractive, why do men only want me for a meal ticket, someone to provide for? This man didn't work and spent his time in the pub - was I just a magnet for down and outs? My husband Harry had told me many times, 'You are nothing to write home about, you look like a bag of bones'. There was nothing Harry liked better than to humiliate and embarrass me in front of his mates. 'Look at my old woman,' he would say, 'the bones on her are like blades, they would cut through you, and her tits are like two fried eggs.' Then he would laugh, looking at his mates to see if they were amused. If I got angry by his comments he would say, 'Ellen, can't you take a joke, sure I was only messing.' Criticism such as this I didn't find funny, especially as I knew he was right.

At that time in my life I was painfully thin, and weighed about seven stone. 'It's like putting clothes on a hanger,' Harry would say; his friends and he would have a good laugh at my expense. I have put on weight since then, and feel better about myself, but still I am nothing like the fifteen year old girl that came to London in 1960 – back then I was fun-loving and confident. I guess circumstances, and life itself, have drained me of those high spirits I once had. Even now I find it difficult to talk to strangers, and would shy away from them. People might find me strange and unfriendly, but that's the way I am. Maybe having been a virtual recluse for so long has something to do with it.

I was now free to go out socially as often as I wished. Katie and Millie would insist on doing my hair and makeup. 'Now go out and enjoy yourself,' they would tell me, and to tell the truth I was getting used to this going out, so much so that I would find myself looking forward to Saturday Nights. I had been trying to persuade Chris to come to the Galtymore with me for months and finally he had agreed to go. 'You can have a drink at the bar,' I told him, as he was still reluctant to dance. At least now I have someone to walk in with, I thought, and I wouldn't have to walk back to my car at 2am on my own. I don't know why I was so nervous around men, feeling none of them were to be trusted, I was tarring all of them with the one brush, and at the same time knowing that that was not right or fair. Having acquired many men friends in the time I had worked in the cafe, men I could trust and feel comfortable talking to, that were kind and caring, yet I did not have the ability or confidence to be sociable outside my working environment.

It was summer time in 1998 that I was finally forced to
come clean and tell my mother about the circumstances of my
marriage's break up, something I had always dreaded. It was
Saturday afternoon, and Mom and I had been out doing our usual
chores, to Hannah's grave in Willesden, where we would water
the flowers, and mother would make sure there wasn't a weed
left in sight, and then very precisely arranging the fresh flowers
we had bought on the way. Then back to the supermarket, for the
shopping. Mom would have a list of things she needed to take back
to Margaret's, where she lived, mainly toiletries and some nice
cakes for Margaret.

As Mom helped me put the shopping away that afternoon,
my brother Chris arrived. He would often call at my house on
Saturdays, knowing Mom would be there, and as always she was
delighted to see him. We would sit outside in the back garden in
the sunshine talking. Mom said, 'Chris, you'll stay and have a
cup of tea with us.' As she went inside to put the kettle on, Chris
said, 'Ellen, have you told her about Harry, and how he doesn't
live here anymore? You need to tell her before someone else does.'
'I know,' I told him, 'but I don't want to upset her, she will be so
disappointed, you know what she is like about such things. The
sacrament of matrimony and so on, she won't be happy.' 'It's not
your fault,' Chris said, 'so just tell her.'

Later that afternoon as Mom was doing her usual tidying up,
she said, 'Ellen, go upstairs and bring me down a couple of Harry's
shirts, and I'll iron them for you.' I had always kept a couple of
Harry's shirts in the house, for this reason – Mom loved ironing
and it made her feel useful, although I felt bad about getting her
to iron shirts that would never be worn. I still went along with the
pretence, though as I handed Mom the shirts, the same two that

she had ironed many times before, Chris interrupted, saying, 'Mother, stop a minute, there is something you need to know. Harry is gone.' 'I know,' mother said, 'sure won't he need his shirts when he gets home. He works so hard, and living away from home so much, it must be tough on the poor devil.' 'No, mother,' Chris said, 'he's gone and he won't be coming back, and I'd say good riddance.' 'What do you mean?' Mom asked, looking at me. 'Ellen, have you had a row or something? Every couple argue from time to time - I am sure he will be back soon.'

I said, 'Chris, leave it, don't say any more,' but my brother wasn't going to give up that easy. He went on to tell Mom, 'Harry had never been any good, he's made her life a misery and they have split up, she's better off without him, it's one less for her to feed and look after.' Mom looked at me, 'Ellen, for the love of God is this true? Marriage is a sacrament, a binding promise to God and each other, till death do us part remember?' Chris mumbled under his breath, 'could be arranged'. I smiled at his comment, as Mom said, 'It's not a laughing matter. Ellen, how are you going to manage on your own? Maria is still young - she'll need her father's guidance.' Mom could only see the good in everyone, and insisted that Harry would be back to his home and family. 'She's a bloody fool if she takes him back this time,' Chris said. 'How many times has Ellen taken him back in the past? Harry has always had other women in his life, and I know that for a fact. I have seen him with other women many times, so mother you can stop preaching the Bible to Ellen, she's done nothing wrong.' I was grateful to my brother for his support. I felt there was enough said, my mother couldn't and didn't accept the situation, I could see she was stressed and worried. 'Don't worry, Mom,' I told her, 'everything will work out for the best, you'll see.'

It was hard for Mom to accept or understand the reason for marriages that go wrong – in her eyes there was no such thing as a failed marriage. Back in Ireland at that time, till death do us part literally meant just that, but that was then. Now, in this modern world, the rules have changed – the slightest disagreement in the marriage now could end in divorce. So I thought Mom should be proud of me, for trying to keep my marriage vows longer than most people would have, in the same circumstances.

I knew Mom would worry more about my soul, than my body; she would have gone home that evening, and prayed to God, asking him to help Ellen and Harry sort out their differences, and save their marriage. I, on the other hand, would be hoping that Mom's prayers wouldn't be answered. I had made up my mind that there would be no going back. I was enjoying my freedom and at last I was happy. I would do almost anything to please my mother, but going back to my old life was asking too much. If only I could explain to her in more detail, she would understand, but talking to my mother about intimate details was out of the question. This kind of information I could never disclose to anyone – the shame and embarrassment was too much for me to handle, people outside the family would think we were like any other married couple, but I knew our marriage was a sham from start to finish. I wished my dad was still alive – he would understand and Mom would listen to him. He would be mad at me for not telling him in the first place; Dad wasn't a man who would accept or tolerate such behaviour from anyone especially his daughter's husband. He would have wanted to hit Harry, and maybe that's what Harry needed, for someone to give him a taste of his own medicine.

I remember one summer Harry, me and the children who were

small at the time, went home on holidays. Nobody in our house had a car, so Dad asked a neighbour Jimmy Sweeney to drive us to town. Being Dad's friend and a neighbour, Jimmy was happy to drive us anywhere we wanted to go. He would take money for petrol and refuse to accept any more than that.

Harry went straight to the pub when we arrived in town; a couple of hours later, with the shopping all done, me and the children were ready to go home. With Harry still in the pub, and reluctant to leave, it would be another hour or so before we finally got on our way back home. Harry had a good few drinks by this time and it showed. Mom had dinner ready for us, Jimmy stayed to eat.

When everyone was finished, Mom and I went clearing off the table, Jimmy got up saying, 'I'll be off now, I have a few jobs to do.' Harry told him, 'You're not going anywhere yet, you are driving me back to town, and after all I am on holiday. I might as well go back on my own for a few more drinks.' 'I can't do that,' Jimmy explained to him. 'I have animals that need seeing to. Sure tomorrow is another day. I will come and pick you up when I have done my jobs tomorrow.'

Harry was not happy and offered to pay. 'I don't want your money,' Jimmy said. With that Harry started swearing at him, 'You good for nothing cunt, you call yourself a driver, what kind of bastard are you, that you won't give a man a lift to the pub.' I was so embarrassed for all of us. Dad was angry. He told Harry, 'That's enough out of you. Jimmy is not a hackney driver, he is doing me a favour and now you have insulted the man. If I were you, I'd apologise.' Harry had never said sorry for anything in his life, and was not about to do now. Instead he continued ranting on and swearing, there was no stopping him. I could see how upset Dad was, and indeed everyone in the house. Dad would have wanted to beat the living daylights out of Harry, but felt he couldn't because of who he was. It was not often I had seen my dad cry, but that evening he went outside and cried with anger and frustration, so I guess my dad always had a fair idea of the kind of man his daughter was married to.

If Dad was still with us now, I felt he would understand and be happy for me and my family; Mom would have listened to Dad. He could influence her, and I am sure he would make her understand; that my marriage break up was the best decision for me. I was worried about my mother – I had expected her to ask loads of questions about Harry and me and at that stage I was prepared to tell her the truth, whatever the questions might be, but she was avoiding the subject completely. It was as if she had never been told anything, she had totally blanked out the conversation that my brother Chris and I had with her months earlier. I always knew Mom wouldn't be happy that I had finally forced Harry to leave, and it was for that reason I felt that lying to her about my husband all these years was my only option. Now Mom was hurt and sad, to the extent that she could not talk about it. I knew Chris was right in saying she should be told; on the other hand I now wished he had not told her – ignorance is bliss, as the saying goes.

Mom did eventually come to terms with what had happened in my marriage, and would even comment how well my family and I were doing, in the absence of a husband and father. She would say, 'Ellen, you look happier now than I've seen you in a long time,' and would go on to say how much things had changed since she was a young woman. 'I could never have managed without your father's help,' she would tell me, but that was in Ireland and mothers did not go out to work. The man of the house was the provider. I would tell Mom how different things are in London, how most women work, there is much more opportunity here for anyone who wants to earn money, and raise a family as well. I would tell her it's not always easy, but lots of women manage.

Harry was still keeping in touch and would visit occasionally. He had been living with Kathy for a couple of years at this stage, but that wasn't going to stop him asking for one more chance. 'We should be together,' he would say. 'I'm not happy with Kathy,' he would tell me. 'You're the only one I've ever truly loved.' Again it was all about him. I would tell him it was out of the question. I would never even consider living with Harry again and I think he knew that, but it wouldn't stop him from trying. I had no interest in sharing my house with anyone; I was happy on my own. I had my uncomplicated social life, I was my own boss and it felt great. I could have gone out on dates but chose not to. My girls would say, 'Mom, you are so boring. The next man that asks you out, just go, don't let your life pass you by.' That's when I decided yes, I should go out on a date, telling myself there is nothing to worry about.

So the next time John, whom I often danced with in the Galtymore, asked if I would go on a date with him, I would say yes. He had been asking me out for some time, and seemed a little surprised that I had finally agreed. I did not want him picking me up from the house. I knew he lived somewhere in Holloway, North London, so I agreed to meet him outside the Gresham dance hall on Holloway Road the next Friday night. I remember being quite excited to begin with, but as the days passed the excitement was replaced with fear, and I really did not want to go. Talking to John in the Galtymore was one thing, but being totally on my own in his company was something else. What would we talk about, maybe he wouldn't like me, and maybe he was married. The thoughts that were going through my head were endless. As I got ready to go out that Friday evening I was a bag of nerves, and wondered why I had agreed to go on this date. My eldest daughter Katie said jokingly, 'Mom, you take my car – you might need it for a quick get-away.' She drove a Fiesta XR2. Deciding it looked better than the Escort van I had at the time, I accepted her offer.

When I got to the Gresham that evening John was already there waiting. 'Thanks for turning up,' he said, leaning into the car and giving me a kiss. As we sat talking in the pub that evening, all I could think about was getting back home. He was a nice man, very talkative, and I could tell he was trying his best to make me feel comfortable. 'There is a nice restaurant around the corner,' he was telling me. 'Are you hungry? Let's finish our drinks, and we will go for something to eat.' But all I could think about was getting home. How sad is that? This man was kind and generous to me, yet I could not relax, I was out of my comfort zone, there was nothing to be nervous about, but I was. As we left the pub that evening, I told John, 'I can't go to the restaurant with you, I've got to go home.' 'Just my luck,' he said, 'anytime I meet someone I like they leave me.' 'I am sorry,' I told him. 'Well at least let me walk you to your car,' he said. As we got to the car that evening I sat in and drove off, leaving poor John standing there on the street; as I drove home I realised how cruel and rude of me to have done that. You're not normal, I told myself.

To this day I sometimes think of that evening and sincerely regret what I did. I had this idea in my head, why should any man like me. I felt there was nothing very likeable about me, I wasn't blessed with good looks or charm of any sort. I guess having suffered rejection for many years, I couldn't take the risk of getting close to anyone. If I don't get involved in a relationship then I can't get hurt or rejected I thought.

I had resigned myself to the fact that I would spend the rest of my life as a single person. My eldest three children were married and had their own homes. Maria, my youngest daughter, was still at home, but I knew in time she would also leave. Then I will be in the house on my own, it's not much to look forward to I thought. I kept myself busy at work; I had my brothers and sisters to visit and Mom whom I would see most days, so I felt happy and content with my life as it was. Why would I want a man in my life? It would only complicate things, and I did not want to go down that path again. I had my health and my children who were very protective of me, in fact sometimes I felt they wanted to wrap me in cotton wool, and put me on the mantelpiece, so they could watch my every move. I often thought how lucky I am to have such a caring family.

Chapter 22

On 31st August 1997 my daughter Katie rang me up. It was a Sunday morning. She told me, 'Lady Diana is dead. She died in a car crash in Paris.' Quickly I turned on the television to check that it was true, and to my disappointment the car in which she had been travelling in was being shown and the circumstances of the accident. I was saddened and shocked by the news, having always admired Princess Diana for her kind loving nature, her charity work, her beauty. She was a royal yet she was her own person, no airs and graces. Women in general could relate to her, she was an inspiration to all. I loved reading about anything to do with Princess Diana, and thought what a terrible loss to the country, the whole world, but especially to her two young sons. The whole country was in mourning.

On the day of her funeral I stood on the A41 with thousands of other people, watching to get one last glimpse of this very special person go by. There were lots of tears as people threw flowers on the hearse carrying her coffin, saying one last farewell to the much loved princess. I sometimes wonder how could this have happened, with all the security and bodyguards, that were engaged to protect her – somebody obviously neglected their duty.

Back home that afternoon I couldn't stop thinking about Diana, how young she was, and how short life can be. I was in my late forties and wondered how much more time I had left. I shouldn't be moping around and living for my family and work. I should be doing things for myself. Up to now I had never been further than north London or Cork, and thought how nice it would be to go to America or Australia. As a young woman I had dreams and ambitions to have a big house, lots of money and my own business. Of course my big house would have enough land to accommodate lots of animals; somehow I had side-stepped most of my ambitions. I guess my expectations in life were set too high for a country girl with little education.

My life hadn't been a complete waste of time. I had four beautiful children, my own house not the mansion I dreamed of, but a nice home nevertheless. At the time I felt quite proud of my achievements, but I knew that given the opportunity I could have done better. Four years had passed since I got my life back on track and I had been happy and contented since then, but now with my children growing up, I was feeling restless. As I lay in bed every night, I would be thinking, where did I go wrong? I would think about all the different places I had lived, and what was happening in my life at the time, sometimes about certain situations that would make me cry. I would be cross with myself, for things I did, or should not have done. I would tell myself go to sleep, stop feeling sorry for yourself. But it was hard to go to sleep with everything that was floating around in my head.

I was not a drinker, but I did have a bottle of whiskey in the house that somebody had given me for Christmas. It would probably have been my neighbour and friend Debbie MacAndrew - she always gave me a bottle of drink every year. I got to thinking if I had a glass of it every night, it would make me sleep, and it did to begin with. I didn't like it very much on its own, and I found it hard to drink, but it was worth the effort to get a good night's sleep. I remember back to when we were children and my dad making punch. He maintained it would cure any illness. It was either that or castor oil in our house if one of us was ill, regardless of the symptoms, that was what was on offer; so we would always

162

choose the punch. But this would be no ordinary whiskey, it would be poteen, a homemade blend; Dad would never be without the stuff. He would keep it hidden away outside around the farmyard; it was for medicinal use only, he would say. Now I was happy it would cure me; I did not have poteen, but whiskey would do. The sugar and boiling water made it easy to drink, and I did start to enjoy it - maybe a little too much as I found myself looking forward to bedtime, and that much needed glass of punch.

As time went by, I found one glass wasn't enough, and increased it to two and then three and so on. I thought is this how some people become alcoholics, is this always how it starts? I was already half way through the second bottle that I had bought, and it still was only a matter of weeks since I drank my first. My drinking was out of control. To some people it wouldn't seem too much, but for me it was heading for disaster. I would be driving to work early in the morning - if the police stopped me it was very likely that I would still be over the limit. I thought if that was to happen maybe I'd be disqualified and lose my licence, and that was unthinkable. Soon I realised that my car, and being allowed to drive it, was much more important to me than my whiskey

After sharing a great part of my life with a man who liked his drink, I knew all about the horrors that came with it. The personality changes, the lack of responsibility, no interest in anything, not even his children. I had learned something from drinking the two bottles of whiskey; how easy it would have been to continue. I had drunk to forget, to blot out incidents from the past that kept me awake at night. Suddenly I realised maybe that was the reason Harry drank so much, was there something in his younger days that he could not cope with, issues that had stayed with him, things he wanted to forget, problems I knew nothing about? We all have a history, something we remember and can smile about, others we want to forget. Having known Harry for thirty years, it made me think how little I really knew about him. During the years I have lived in England, mainly mixing and working with Irish people, I've been told so many sad stories from people, who, like me, were reared in this so called holy Ireland. The cruelty plus the secrecy and young men and women not knowing who their parents were. They had no identity.

A customer once told me a very sad tale. I knew him pretty well. Jack would come to the café once or twice a day. As I sat talking to him, he was telling me about the village where he came from in Ireland and in the same breath he said, 'Ellen, my sister had me.' Shocked and a little confused by his statement, I had to think to analyse what he had told me. I tried to explain to him that this lady was in fact his mother, not his sister. He continued to tell me how he had been told who his mother was. 'It was only last year,' he said, he was at a function here in London and met a couple of neighbours from home, 'who asked how my mother was'. I told them, 'My mother died three years ago.' 'No,' she said, 'that was your grandmother. I'm talking about Mary, your mother.'

He told me how shocked and angry he was that he hadn't been told by a member of his family. 'Don't get me wrong,' he said, 'I had a happy childhood and I am grateful to them for that, but I should have been told as a child. I'm in my late forties now, and feel my whole life has been a lie. Where do I go from here?' he asked. 'Do I go home and confront Mary the woman who I thought was my sister or do I let sleeping dogs lie?' Unable to advise him I said, 'You're one of many through Ireland that's in similar situations; your mother must have had her reasons for not telling you.'

When I got home that evening I thought how lucky and privileged I was to have such a caring Mom and Dad, while others feel sad and unwanted, ashamed of who they are. I thought a lot about Jack in the days that followed, and the predicament he found himself in. There were many people throughout Ireland like Jack. Having a baby outside marriage was a terrible embarrassment back then; it was all about what the neighbours would say, and how sinful this was, the local priest would have to be told. He would be the person most people feared; those young girls were naive and innocent, and knew nothing about the facts of life, yet because they were pregnant, they would be removed from society. This would be usually arranged by the local priest. The poor deluded parents felt they had no choice but to accept their young daughter's fate. Allowing her to be removed from her home and placed in an institution for unmarried mothers, which is where many of those young girls would spend the rest of their life. The baby would be adopted often without the mother's consent, their families disowning them, their dreams and ambitions snatched away.

I often wondered how these women coped with their plight; some committed suicide, and I can understand why. All they had left to look forward to was a bed and some food, and in return, they were made to work, cleaning floors, and scrubbing rich people's dirty washing. In my mind, it takes two to make a baby. Some man had taken advantage of a young girl's innocence but sadly he was not man enough to own up to his responsibility. Pretty selfish I think. Society deprived many young women of their freedom. Having a family, all the things most women take for granted, they paid a huge price for their so called sin. The God I know and loved didn't inflict such punishment on those young mothers; the atrocity lies solely with religious clergy and the community.

Chapter 23

I started dating James in February 1997; he was someone I had known for a long time initially through my work. He came from the North of Ireland; he was someone I could have a laugh and a joke with. Then one day he said, 'Can I ask your advice about something?' I said, 'Sure, ask away.' 'I fancy one of the girls that works here, I'm a bit shy in asking her out. What should I do?' 'Just ask her out,' I told him. 'She can only say no or maybe yes.' I did not even ask him which one it was that he wanted to go out with.

Then one night my brother Chris and I were in the Crown pub in Cricklewood having a drink, and listening to music, when James appeared, offering to buy us a drink. Chris accepted and invited James to join us, as he seemed to be on his own. Later I told Chris I was going to the Galtymore. 'Are you sure you don't want to come with me?' I asked. 'No,' he said, 'I won't bother tonight, but you wait until I've finished my pint and I'll walk with you.' 'It is only a few hundred yards,' I said, 'I'll be fine on my own, you stay and finish your pint.' James said, 'Ellen, if you don't mind walking with me, I am going to the Galty too.' As we got to the club James insisted on paying for me to get in. I told him no but he was adamant. Inside the hall he said, 'I hope you don't go away and leave me on my own, at least stay and have a drink with me.' I agreed telling him just one drink.

As we stood chatting he asked, 'Do you remember a few weeks ago, I told you I fancied one of the girls in your café? Well it's you!' I laughed saying, 'You must be joking, you're years younger than me. No way, forget it.' 'Don't be like that,' he said. 'What's twelve years? Anyway you don't look as old as you say.' 'And it's still no,'

I said. I said to him, 'James, one day you will meet someone your
own age and maybe want a family. I've got my family already as
you know, so me and you just wouldn't work.'

I knew already that James had been in a relationship that had
ended two years before, and he had a stepdaughter. 'She is more
like my own daughter,' he told me, 'and with my one and your
four, that's a big enough family for me.' James was saying all the
right things, and was adamant that the age difference didn't
matter but for me it did matter. Over the next few months I would
see James most days; he would buy me presents. 'I am not going
to give up on you,' he would say. I had never thought of him in a
romantic way, I had looked on him as a friend, nothing more, then
one evening he called, telling me he was going somewhere special
at the weekend, and needed a partner. 'Please will you come with
me?' he pleaded. I agreed telling him it would be a one off date,
but it wasn't and fifteen years on, we are still together, though the
romance hasn't always been sunshine and roses - we have had a
few fall outs along the way.

To begin with my children were happy for me, and they seemed
to like James - that was until they realised he might become a
permanent fixture. After having my undivided attention all their
lives, I don't think they cherished the thought of sharing me with
anyone. They would tell me, 'He's not good enough for you, Mom.'
They had put me on such a high pedestal that no one could live up
to their expectations. And it was not just my family, James' family
were even more critical, and disapproved of me completely,
especially his two sisters. One of them lived in England and
would tell James, 'Find somebody your own age, she will never
have a family for you.' His family who lived in Ireland were even
more controlling and would tell James, 'She's a divorcee with four

children. Why are you interested in someone like her?'

The criticisms were endless. These people had never met me and knew nothing about me, but had made it abundantly clear that I wasn't welcome in their family; his family would often ring him on his mobile when we were together. I could always get the gist of the conversation, and what really annoyed me was that James would never disagree with anything they said; he would never defend himself or me, or tell them to mind their own business, this is the girl I want to be with so back off. I wanted him to speak up for me; after all we had been together for nearly a year. His family rejection caused arguments; they were driving a wedge between us, and succeeded but all James would say was, 'Ellen take no notice of them, you have to listen to thunder.'

I soon realised that James wasn't as attentive as he used to be, and wondered if he was having doubts about being with me, the relationship didn't seem to be going anywhere – not that I was interested in marriage – but the age gap had always concerned me. And I felt now that he's got his doubts too, I told myself you have got to end this. I knew I would miss James; we had had such a good time during the past year.

I think my mother was happy that James was not around anymore; she worried about the religious aspect. She liked James as a person but was concerned that I would get too involved. 'You know, Ellen,' she would say, 'in the eyes of God you are still a married woman, regardless of whether your husband is with you or not.'

James still kept in touch with me. 'We can at least be friends,' he said, and he would sometimes call to the house, send me flowers, and would ring me regularly. I missed having him around, having someone to go out with at the weekend. I wondered why James was still so attentive, his family had got what they wanted, we weren't together anymore, so why was he so keen to know what I was doing. He would ring me on a Saturday evening and ask, 'Are you going out tonight, and who is going with you?' I guess James was doing what his family wanted, pleasing them and not himself. He was a man in his forties and was still being controlled by his family. Family are important to all of us, but at that age I would have thought, who we go out with is our business and nobody else's. I wasn't having much luck with the men in my life, but at least this time it was James' inability to tell his family where to go, that caused the rift between us.

Mid-way through 1997 my dear mother discovered a lump on her breast. She showed it to my sister Margaret, who immediately suspected it could be cancer and rang to tell me of her suspicion. 'I am taking her straight to the doctors,' she said. I was really worried. As Margaret put the phone down, I felt numb; it can't be cancer, I told myself. Mom had never done a wrong thing in her life. God wouldn't let something like this happen to our mother, she is the best and kindest person in the world. I convinced myself that she must have knocked herself, or it might be a cyst. Mom was a keen gardener, and there was nothing she liked better than being outside with her spade, digging, weeding plants. Margaret's garden looked perfect. That's what it is, I thought, she must have fallen, that lump will disappear in a few days. I wouldn't allow myself to think it was anything more than that.

Within a couple of weeks she had an appointment to see a cancer specialist in hospital in Hampstead. I prayed that it wasn't the dreaded cancer, but to my horror the diagnosis was bad: Mom had breast cancer. The specialist had given us some hope; he said, 'There is going to be no nasty surgery. Your mother is eighty three; at her age, everything slows down, and this cancer will also be so slow growing that it will never kill her. Don't worry about it, Mrs Kelly, come back and see me in six months.' Mother seemed fine physically so we all got on with our lives as usual; after all, the doctor must know, so we clung on to what he had told us. Mom wasn't going to die, and we tried not to mention that word again; though it would remain in the back of my mind, I tried not to think, about it too much.

Mom seemed healthy, doing all the things that she would normally do. She had always been an active person, and that hadn't changed. I would still pick her up on Saturday morning, we would drive around, do some shopping and so on; sometimes I would have my grandson with me and though he was only two, Mom would have him sitting on her lap, teaching him how to bless himself. She would often make me laugh at some of her comments, as we drove around. 'Ellen,' she would say, 'why is that man wearing a woman's dress?' I would explain to her that it was their religion. She often found it hard to understand why we had so many churches in this country. 'What's the need for them all?' she would say. 'We have only got two different churches in Ireland, one for the Catholics and one for the Protestants.' So every church we would pass she would say, 'Ellen, is that one of ours, or is it the opposition?' I would laugh at her remarks, she was so funny, so witty at times. My children knew about their grandmother's illness, but as I wasn't making a big deal about it, they didn't either; they all thought the world of their Nan, and would hate the thought of losing her.

As usual that summer we went back to Ireland on holiday with Mom. She was very happy here, but she loved going home, seeing all her old friends and neighbours. There wasn't that many of them left anymore; some had died, others had moved to different parts of the country to be with their own families. There would still be lots of relatives dotted around Cork to visit though. One person in particular I always tried to spend some time with was my aunty 'Baby' as she was called, such a wonderful person and I loved her dearly. Mom and she had been great friends and would write to each other regularly. My dad on the other hand had never got on with his sister 'Baby', always civil to each other, but that was it, they weren't close, like a brother and sister should be. I think Dad was a little jealous of his sister – she had married well into a big farm, and although she had lost her husband at a young age – he had a heart attack and had died in her arms, leaving her with three young children – she still managed to run the farm successfully with some hired help.

It was nearly a year since Mom first found the cancerous lump in her breast, and already it had grown to nearly three times the size; it was now visible through her clothes and had changed in colour. Margaret had managed to get an urgent appointment with a consultant who seemed surprised that it had grown so much so quickly. 'It will have to be removed,' he told us. 'I will arrange to have you admitted as soon as possible, Mrs Kelly. We will also be removing your breast.' We did not know how Mother would feel about that, but after explaining the procedure to her, she did not feel too bothered about it. I am sure she was worried, and was putting on a brave face for our benefit; that was typical of Mom who would never complain – any anxiety she had she would keep to herself.

The day of her surgery was a worrying time for all the family, but the operation went well, and we were all pleased that it was over. I had real hope now that she would make a full recovery.

She was getting better every day. I would go to see her on my lunch break, and again late evening. Mum would say, 'Ellen I am a bloody nuisance to you all', but that was something our mother could never be; she had seven children and now all of us had children of our own, and so mother was never short of visitors. She would have a big smile for every familiar face as they approached her bed. Knowing how deaf Mom was, I knew she would not be able to have a conversation with other patients in her ward, that is why I felt the need to go and visit her at bedtime, in case there was anything wrong, she might need something, and being the sort of person she was, and not wanting to bother the hospital staff, she would manage rather than ask for help.

Two weeks after surgery Mother was up and walking around, with her drains and drips all removed. She was feeling great, I was so pleased for her, she would be fine. Even the doctor had said, 'Mrs Kelly, you have made a remarkable recovery, so I feel you are ready to go home tomorrow morning.' Mom was so delighted to be going home, so excited. 'Margaret will be in later,' she said, 'you might ring her and tell her to bring in my clothes. I would like to have everything ready for the morning, so as not to keep Margaret waiting when she comes to collect me.' I knew there would be no need for my bedtime visit that day, but I still went. I told Mom, 'I won't be in tomorrow, I will see you at Margaret's tomorrow evening.'

Just before I left the hospital that night, a male nurse came into the ward. I was surprised to see him coming towards my mother's bed. I asked what the problem was, telling him she was being discharged in the morning. He told me the blood clinic had requested that 'we give your mother this medication'. I tried to question the nurse further, saying that the doctor hadn't mentioned anything about this. 'Why does my mother need this?' 'I am only a nurse,' he said, 'doing as I've been told.' As I left the hospital that night, I thought they must know what they are doing, she would be fine, but sadly things were far from fine. My sister Mary got a phone call, to tell her Mother had a bleed in the night.

As we got to her ward we found her bed gone. We just stood there panicking, where is Mom, we thought. Another patient who was in the bed opposite said, 'Mrs Kelly was moved out of this ward in the night. I got up to go to the toilet and noticed all the blood on your mother's sheets and the floor. So I rang the bell. A nurse came and immediately drew the curtains; when I came back from the toilet, your mother had gone. I hope she is all right.'

Mother had been moved to the high dependency ward; there were doctors and nurses around her bed. A doctor was telling us, 'Your mother had a bleed in the night, she is not very well at the moment, and we will be taking her back to theatre to drain all this blood.' She had pockets of blood all around her shoulders and where her breast had been. I was so shocked and angry I couldn't speak. I wanted to say this is your fault, you insisted on giving her that medication yesterday evening, I told you she did not need it, she should be going home today, and now look at what has happened. Mom was very weak and not talking to us; we knew this would be a terrible setback for her. How could the hospital staff be so negligent, incompetent? They didn't seem to be accepting any responsibility for what had happened, in fact they were saying very little, but I truly believed that whatever they had given her the previous night was responsible. How could my mother be well and fit, getting all her belongings together the night before, she could not wait to get home, and be nearly at death's door a few hours later? Mom was very weak and unresponsive through the next couple of days, but thank God she did eventually gain her strength and was well enough to come home.

Margaret had hired a retired nurse to look after Mother while she went to work. The nurse would help her with personal care, and keep her company. Though Mom seemed well, she had never recovered completely from her ordeal. She would say to Margaret, 'Is this the beginning of the end?' To hear that statement was heart-breaking. It had only been a few months since her surgery and already more lumps had appeared under her arm; the cancer had spread, and at that point I knew that within a short time I would lose my mother. I tried very hard to keep my emotions hidden but it was so very hard. At times Mom would ask Margaret, 'Is Ellen all right, she looks as if she's been crying.' Margaret would tell her, 'It's because she misses James, as you know they fell out.'

I could not tell my children. I thought what's the point in making them miserable. I hoped and prayed that Mom would survive, for at least for a few more years. I would still call to collect her on Saturday morning, as I had been doing for a couple of years. She would always be dressed and waiting for me. Our route would take the same direction, to the cemetery, visiting brother Chris, shopping and then back to my house for lunch. I wondered how many more Saturdays my Mom would be sitting in the car beside me, as we drove around. I tried to look happy and light hearted, but I was crying inside. I just could not bear the thought of losing her. It was a Saturday morning in November; Mom wasn't up and ready to go out. I went into her bedroom. She said, 'Ellen, I hope you don't mind, but I'm not feeling too well,

I won't go out today.' At that moment I knew, this really was the beginning of the end. I made some excuse, telling her I would be back later. I could not hold back the tears any longer, I was inconsolable. Soon after Mom developed a cough; the cancer had spread to her lungs; there was nothing anyone could do for her, and my heart really was broken.

Chapter 24

It was Easter weekend in 2000 when Mom was again admitted to hospital; this time it was Central Middlesex Park Royal, and though they tried their best to get her chest infection under control with intravenous antibiotics, if we got to her a few days earlier, the doctor was telling us, we may have been able to save her. Sadly my beautiful mother had passed away on 10 April 2000 with all her seven children around her. I couldn't stop crying; my whole world had fallen apart - the only person in the whole world that I loved and trusted had gone, and I was numb with grief. I was blaming myself, the hospital in Hampstead, whom I felt had neglected her so badly. Was it that bleed that had shortened her life? I should have insisted that evening when she was given that blood thinning medication, that her blood should be checked and properly monitored, but I hadn't, and now I had lost her. Friends would say to me your mother was a good age, at eighty six, which didn't help, because if mother was 100 it would not have made me feel any better - the sense of loss would have been the same.

Dad had passed away in 1996 and though I missed him terribly, I did not have the same sense of grief. Maybe it was because Dad's quality of life was non-existent. He had been paralysed and blind for many years. Now twelve years on I still find it hard to talk about my mother.

James had been very supportive to me during that time. He had turned up at the hospital a few days before Mom died; we had been taking it in turns to sit up with her every night. She was pleased to see James, but had an even bigger welcome for my then ex-husband Harry. I think even at that stage, she secretly hoped that we would get back together. Mom was buried beside her husband back in Ireland, and I hope and pray that they are happy together in heaven.

I don't know how James and I got back together; he had continued to help and support me through those dark days, but I know one thing – I would never have got back with James, had my mother not died and that would have been a shame, because he's a good man . Gone are the days when I dreaded hearing that key in the door, my stomach churning and my nerves on edge, gone are the nights when I dreaded going to bed with a man whom I know cared nothing for me, who made me feel worthless. I have now regained my confidence and no longer see men as a threat.

There are good men out there and I would say to any woman, who's been treated badly by her partner, don't wait in the hope that things will get better, because they rarely do. Find the courage and strength – there is always a way, it is just a matter of finding it. I wasted many years hoping and praying that things would get better. I forgot that in the meantime things were passing me by. Don't waste your life being miserable; we have only got one shot at it. Everyone deserves to be happy, and it's up to us to make that happen; don't wait until you're too old to make a difference.

James and I have been living together for the past twelve years. During that time we've had two, maybe three arguments – not bad I think. Sadly there's a downside to our relationship: I'm not allowed to practise my Catholic religion – or so I've been told. After we had been together for about a year, I went to confession and told the priest that I was living with James, who is not my husband. I don't know what I expected him to say, maybe I thought he would be sympathetic, after all I felt I deserved a bit of happiness. 'You're committing adultery,' he told me. 'You're going against the Catholic Religion. I can't give you absolution as long as you're cohabiting with this man.' As if that wasn't bad enough he continued to tell me, 'I must also forbid you from receiving the Sacraments, though you may still come to the church.'

Leaving the church that day, feeling let down and shocked, it wasn't the reception I had hoped for. I had been banned from practising my religion. I am doomed I thought, even God doesn't want me. I discussed it with my family. My brother Chris suggested I get my marriage annulled, which costs money, takes a long time and involves the whole family. I don't believe in annulment and thought I have had five children within my marriage. How could that be dismissed as though it had never happened? It's a sham, I thought, a money making racket. After getting over the initial disappointment I thought a lot about religion and how things have been changed over the years.

I remember as a young girl going to church back in Ireland, at Easter time, every family in the parish was expected to make a yearly offering to the church. People would give what they could afford. On the following Sunday the priest would call out everyone's name and what they had given, leaving the people who gave little or nothing at all humiliated and embarrassed. I did not think much about it at the time. But now that I think about it, that was very unkind and I can only assume that it was a way of getting more money out of poor people.

I also think about our priests, and why they're not allowed to marry - that is another manmade ruling, as there was a time when priests were married and had families of their own. The Vatican I believe put a stop on that, solely for financial reasons. In my opinion, a priest who is married would be more understanding, with a better insight into what can happen in a relationship. How can he understand the difficulties we have, if he has never experienced such things? After all it says in the Bible, Jesus said, 'go forth and multiply'. I don't think he excluded Priests, Bishops and Cardinals. These people at the top should look at the wider picture and realise that religious ministers are also human beings with the same needs as the rest of us.

It saddens me to think about all the scandalous actions I read about in the papers, or see on television documentaries, about our Priests, Cardinals and other religious leaders, their abusers and the people who cover up their crimes. I am glad Mom had passed away before these atrocities came to light; she would have been mortified, a true believer, our religious leaders were so very important in her life, there would be no room for doubt. I think back then we all felt the same, our priests were someone we looked up to; for my mother she would have seen them as her stepping stone to heaven, someone to guide us and to forgive us for our failings and our imperfections.

So when I looked for forgiveness on that day in confession expecting help, maybe a solution, I certainly didn't expect to be banished after that day, and on reflection, I felt like it was a case of, don't do as I do, do as I say. I know we have thousands of good priests; it's a shame that a few who have lost their way have tarnished our catholic faith with long lasting effects. I have noticed a change in the congregation every Sunday dwindling away and remembering the times when every church in the parish would be full to overflowing, at mass time, men on one knee outside the door because there was no room inside. Something has gone badly wrong and it saddens me to see it. Even my own family rarely goes to church nowadays. For me Sunday wouldn't feel right if I hadn't been to church. Something would be missing; it would be like I had missed the whole day.

Back in the 60s when I lived in St Cuthbert's Road, there was a Methodist church at the end of the road. I would wake on Sunday mornings to the sound of the church bells. I loved hearing that sound and there were many churches around the area ringing their bells. I rarely hear them anymore and often wonder why. I feel we all need someone or something to believe in, whatever our religious beliefs may be or which church we belong to; after all, we all share the same God. I feel religion is what kept me sane, during those many unhappy years, and I am proud of who I am, thanks to my parents, because they taught me how to survive and appreciate what I had.

Nowadays, people don't appreciate anything; everyone wants more, things they don't really need and often ill afford, greed has set in and that's not a nice quality in a person. I remember a time when having a roof over my head and enough food to feed the family made me happy. Nowadays I expect much more, nice clothes, jewellery and a nice car - I go with the flow. I don't need many of the possessions that I spend money on and it's only when I see someone walking around in ill-fitting clothes, and others' cast-offs that it hits home to me and I remember how things were. I see young men and women standing on street corners, begging, even going through bins, outside take-aways, in the hope that somebody might have left a few chips or the remains of a burger or maybe a piece of chicken. Then there is Hill sixteen, as many people call it - it's a piece of wasteland off Cricklewood Lane, where men and occasionally women would sit with their cans of beer; whatever the weather, that was their place.

I look at myself and people around me and think what we

waste, how selfish we have all become when we could help these poor individuals; they shouldn't have to live like that, but we just can't be bothered. On occasions I would give them money, and friends would say to me, 'Why are you wasting your money on them, they will only buy drinks with it; you are not doing them any favours' they would tell me. I don't look at it like that and say maybe they are hungry. Put your hand in your pocket and don't be mean, at least give them the choice. I know there are lots of good people, who dedicate their lives to helping others and sadly there can be many more who could help but won't, myself included. These poor people are looked upon as tramps, a waste of space, worthless. It is so easy to forget that they are somebody's son or daughter that has fallen on hard times; we don't know their circumstances and too many of us don't want to know.

Chapter 25

My partner and I were recently invited to a lavish dinner dance in the Crown Hotel in Cricklewood. After parking our car a few streets away, we walked towards the hotel and sitting there on the pavement was a young man with his hand stretched out in the hope that someone would give him money. I could not help but notice him as he sat there in front of a supermarket that was still open. I wanted to stop to give him some change, but I knew what my partner James would say, 'Come on Ellen, we're running late, you are too soft, keep your money, he should go to work like the rest of us.' It's not that James is a mean person, it's just that he doesn't understand and can't put himself in their situation like I can. That short stint on the street, back in 1970 taught me something – how to be compassionate towards our street friends – and I am glad of the experience now, though I wasn't too impressed at the time.

As we sat down for our lavish four course meal that night, I couldn't stop thinking about the young man outside, sitting on that cold pavement in the middle of November, how cold he must be, wearing those skimpy clothes. I thought how happy it would make me if only I could give him a plateful of this beautiful well prepared food. I was not enjoying mine; it may as well have been cold chips. Looking around me I could see evidence of wealth; I had even noticed on my way in a new Bentley parked outside the door. I thought how tragic and unfair life can be. I'm sure the man who drove the Bentley was a kind and generous man, but like the rest of us he wouldn't notice or realise how bad things can be for some people. I did not enjoy the night, I felt out of my comfort zone and would have been happier in the rough and tumble pub around the corner, where many of our street friends go, in the hope that someone would buy them a pint.

One day I hope God will guide my hand to the winning lottery numbers, so I can buy a mansion to put all these people in so they could have a warm comfortable home like the rest of us, it would be a privilege. A great many of these poor people are Irish, many of them have spent most of their lives in London, coming here in the 50s or 60s. They would have worked hard many hours a day, earned good money only to hand it over to the landlord of some pub. To support their drinking habits they would eat in cafés, live in shabby rooms and that was their lives. Many of these men would lose contact with their families back home, because they would either be at work or drunk - no time for family life, their parents, brothers and sisters anxious and worried about where they were or what had happened to them. There would be no such thing as putting money by for a rainy day - they drank what they had until next pay day with no sense of achievement or making a better life for themselves. They lived a lonely life and many died in their rented rooms on their own.

I don't mean to criticise the Irish, being one myself, and I am well aware that it could be any one of us, who turned to drink for comfort with their only friend being the landlord behind the bar. It's not just the Irish who fell by the wayside; there are people from all over the world, in the same situation, for one reason or another. I am very proud of some of my countrymen, who came to England with little money, no friends or family to help them, their only asset was ambition and with hard work and dedication they made their mark in the country. Now they are some of the biggest and best in the construction industry, and many others who came to this country with great expectations of riches, but sadly not much since.

My husband got many opportunities to do well, he was a good worker when the notion took him, but he wasn't consistent, feeling that he had to get rid of one wage packet before he earned another. I tried hard to steer him in the right direction, but we seemed to be on different wavelengths. Eventually I gave up and the pub landlord won. The drink was too high on his list of priorities for me to cope with and I resigned myself to the fact that though I would always have to work I could never achieve anything more than making a living. I sometimes think that if only I could go back and start again with the knowledge and experience I have had over the years, I feel that I could have achieved much more. I could have been the one driving that Bentley that was parked outside the Cricklewood hotel recently. Maybe I wasn't meant to be rich, I should be happy with what I've got, a lovely family and a partner who cares about me, and that's a lot more than some people have, so I tell myself, don't be selfish Ellen, be grateful, what more is there.

My greatest ambition now is that when I leave this world I'll go to heaven to be with Mom and Dad and my son, and many others, relatives and friends. So I hope when I get to those pearly gates that God will look on me kindly and maybe allow me a little concession under the circumstances of how I've lived my life. I know some of our priests would think I am a bad person, an adulteress and sinful but in my heart I don't consider myself a sinful person. So now I'm hoping the man at the top, God, will agree – after all He helped me in the past, maybe he should have a word with his workforce and tell them to be more forgiving and understanding; everything isn't black and white and it's not always possible to follow the rules laid out for us.

My ex-husband Harry now lives alone and at times I feel a bit sorry for him. He knows I will always be there for him when he needs me. For some reason I still feel responsible for him and I don't expect that to change. His children also help him and keep in touch as he is their dad and they have a certain amount of respect for him thus I wouldn't have it any other way. The past is now a memory and neither my children nor I have any animosity towards him. I can't altogether blame Harry and I must accept some of the responsibility as it takes two and I allowed him to bully me and to treat me like something he had picked up on the end of his shoe – it was up to me to say enough. The reason why I didn't was religion and a certain amount of weakness on my part. I have long since forgiven Harry, but forgetting is much harder and I don't suppose I ever will. I feel as I am writing this that somehow it's betrayal and I don't mean it to be. I would never want to hurt Harry or cause him any heartache – that is not my intention.

I feel very privileged nowadays, the children spoil me and if Harry had treated us better, he would still be right beside me, getting spoiled as well. I have done some travelling over the years, all paid for by my family. They have taken me to Italy, Spain, Cyprus, Greece and not forgetting New York. I loved it there and travelled first class, so I consider myself well-travelled for somebody that had never been outside London up to ten years ago. But my greatest love of all is County Cork; all the places I've been and the countries that I intend to see in the future, would never come close to my old home in Ireland. I spend a lot more time there nowadays; my children don't really need me anymore, and I'm free to come and go as I please, in fact they encourage it.

CHAPTER 25

I recently went back to Cork for a few days, accompanied by my children and grandchildren. My brother Frank was happy to let us stay in our old home, which has been extended and refurbished to a high standard. It looks different now, but it was wonderful to be able to stay there. The memories of a wonderful childhood all came flooding back. My grandchildren played around the fields and the farmyard, just as I and my brothers and sisters had done as kids. The planks of wood across the fence, which made a fabulous see-saw, we spent many hours playing on that simple plank of wood – it wasn't like it is now, we had no computer games or any other toys; we made our own games, and had more fun with them than anything Mom or Dad could have bought us.

Now as I watch my grandchildren enjoying themselves, having more fun with the simple things, than they would ever have in London, with all their expensive toys and games, listening to them laughing as they pushed one another into the mud, having water fights, not once did I hear them complain or look for their computer games. They would roll themselves down the high field in front of our house to see which one got to the bottom first; of course they destroyed their clothes with grass stains, but it was worth it, listening to the laughter coming out of them. It was the same every day: the children would always find something to amuse themselves. As soon as breakfast was eaten they went off. Sometimes their parents would wonder where they were, but as they were together we didn't worry much. I would say to their parents, that's what you did when I brought you home on holidays, and when you lot got hungry, you would always head for home, so don't worry no harm will come to them.

I will be eternally grateful to my brother Frank and his wife Eileen for allowing us to stay in our old home, for those few days;

they made us welcome in all sorts of ways. A year on we are still talking about the good time we had, a memory we will always treasure. My family think I am a sentimental old fool and I guess they may be right; my brothers and sisters have long since moved on in life, and rarely visit the old farmhouse in the South of Ireland, but for me it's still my home. I sometimes wonder why that is and think maybe because I left home at such a young age – at fifteen most children would still be with their mom and dad. I didn't have to leave; Mom and Dad were upset when I chose to, but I got the opportunity and going to London at that time seemed so appealing. Now I seem to spend a lot of time trying to turn the clock back and how wonderful that would be.

As I stand in the field in front of that old house, in my mind's eye, I can still see all of us as children, playing, laughing, fighting and sometimes crying, Mum would be standing at the front door laughing at our antics, Dad often sitting inside would shout at Mom, and say, 'Mary, have you got no control over them children, one of them is going to get hurt,' but Mom rarely stopped us. I think secretly she would have liked to join in the fun. Being an only child with very protective parents, she wouldn't have had the same kind of childhood as we had.

As adults when we were home on holiday, we all got together as a kind of reunion and that's when the real fun would start. Water fights were our favourite, sometimes with Mom joining in; anything that would hold water was used, even if we had to empty bottles and milk containers down the sink. We would all end up soaked as would the house, but it did not matter as we would all chip in with the mopping up and of course someone would have to go and replace the milk that was poured down the sink.

James is not a person who goes drinking for the sake of it.

Once a week would be enough for him, usually on a Saturday night when we would be out together. James would never go out socially without me, so history definitely won't repeat itself. I would like to see the Government make changes in our drinking laws, and make pub landlords take more responsibility for their customers. At the moment these publicans seem to ply drink on anyone who has the money to pay for it, whatever their condition. There doesn't seem to be any cut off point, and we all know of the high crime rate, fuelled by over drinking. I am all for going out and having a drink and socialising with friends and family but I detest being in the company of people who have drank so much that they become angry, aggressive and sometimes even crude – that's when I want to distance myself from their foul mouth and shit talk.

My brother Chris moved back to Ireland three years ago with his wife Angela and I do miss him. He is not at my beck and call any more, not a phone call away if anything goes wrong, or if something needs fixing. Chris had been my ally since I arrived in London, and it's not the same without him, but everyone has to move on, and I should too.

James has asked me to marry him and I have said yes. I would have liked to be married in a church but that's not possible. My family are happy for me and I hope Mom and Dad will give me their blessing from up above. The wedding will be back in Cork and we are both looking forward to the occasion with our family and friends around us, so maybe there will be a happy ending. I surely hope so.

I am happy and content with my life as it is now. I have everything and want for nothing. Bad things have happened to me in the past. I've been beaten, raped and violated in many ways but that's life and as the song goes, Hard Times Come Again No More.

Lightning Source UK Ltd.
Milton Keynes UK
UKOW03f2144211014

240457UK00005B/586/P

9 780957 380967